DANCING
WITH THE *DUSHMAN*

Dancing with the *Dushman*:
Command Imperatives for the Counter-Insurgency Fight in Afghanistan

By
Lieutenant-Colonel Ian Hope, MSC, CD
Commanding Officer
Task Force Orion
February-August 2006

CANADIAN DEFENCE ACADEMY PRESS

Canadian Defence Academy Press
PO Box 17000 Stn Forces
Kingston, Ontario   K7K 7B4

Produced for the Canadian Defence Academy Press
by 17 Wing Winnipeg Publishing Office.
WPO30335

Cover Photo: Courtesy of Captain Jay Adair 2 PPCLI
Photo depicts acting OC Adair giving quick attack orders to his Platoon Commanders: David Ferris, Conrad von Finklestein and Sean Ivanko in Pashmul, May 2006

Inside Front & Back Cover Maps: Courtesy of the Mapping and Charting Establishment

Library and Archives Canada Cataloguing in Publication

Library and Archives Canada Cataloguing in Publication

Hope, Ian
Dancing with the Dushman : command imperatives for the counter-insurgency fight in Afghanistan / by Ian Hope.

Issued by Canadian Defence Academy.
ISBN 978-0-662-47817-1 (bound).--ISBN 978-0-662-47818-8 (pbk)
Cat. no.: D2-221/1-1-2008E (bound) -- Cat. no.: D2-221/1-2-2008E (pbk)

1. Afghan War, 2001- --Participation, Canadian. 2. Afghan War, 2001- --Personal narratives, Canadian. 3. Canada--Armed Forces--Afghanistan. 4. Command of troops. 5. Afghanistan. I. Canadian Defence Academy I. Title II. Title: Command imperatives for the counter-insurgency fight in Afghanistan.

FC543.H66 2008   958.104'7   C2008-980094-X

Printed in Canada.

1 3 5 7 9 10 8 6 4 2

Table of Contents

Foreword

I am delighted to introduce *Dancing with the Dushman: Command Imperatives for the Counter-Insurgency Fight in Afghanistan*, which represents the latest volume from the Canadian Defence Academy (CDA) Press. More specifically it is the 41st book published by CDA Press since its creation in 2005. As such, the Press is well on its way to capturing operational experience that can be used in our professional development institutions. After all, this book, like many of those before it and those still in press, are an integral component of our Strategic Leadership Writing Project, which is designed to (a) create a distinct and unique body of Canadian leadership literature and knowledge that will assist leaders at all levels of the Canadian Forces to prepare themselves for operations in a complex security environment, and (b) inform the public with respect to the contribution of Canadian Forces service personnel to Canadian society and international affairs.

Dancing with the Dushman is in many ways the epitome of the type of book the Press strives to publish. Written by Lieutenant-Colonel (LCol) Ian Hope, commander of Task Force (TF) Orion, Canada's first battle group deployed into Kandahar Province in Afghanistan, it captures the challenges, trials and tribulations of a commander at war. His dramatic experiences, valuable insights and exciting narrative provide a wealth of knowledge to those who practice or study the profession of arms. It clearly identifies the difficulties of commanding troops in combat; fighting an insurgency and dealing with an alien culture and multi-national coalition. The lessons contained provide vicarious experience that will assist all ranks, as well as non-military persons better understand leadership, command and conflict.

In closing, I wish to reiterate that *Dancing with the Dushman* is an important new addition to the CDA Press list of titles. It adds to the sparse body of contemporary Canadian military operational leadership literature. As such, I believe that it will provide valuable insight to all those who serve in, and equally those who interact with, the profession of arms in Canada.

Colonel Bernd Horn
Chairman, CDA Press

Prologue

August 3rd 2006

I cannot tell you exactly how many intense combat actions were fought during our seven months; over fifty, ranging from distant Maruf, Garmser, Musa Qalah, to just outside of our patrol base in Zhelay. I cannot tell you how many decisions were taken by me in all those days, or on any given one. But I can tell you unequivocally that the hardest decision I had to make during the whole tour came in the late afternoon of 3rd August 2006. It occurred as I stood in the hot sun on the pebbled bottom of the wide and shallow wadi that is the Arghandab River, beside the remaining Light Armour Vehicles (LAVs), Light Utility Vehicle ("G-Wagons") and Nyalas (RG-31 light patrol vehicles), smoking a cigar and looking with hatred at the buildings 600 metres away in the bazaar in Bayanzi, where the Taliban had massed and fought from. Three kilometres to our north, B Company was having good success hammering a Taliban group that they had trapped inside of a compound in the northern part of Pashmul. Working alongside 100 Afghan National Police (ANP), they had forced about 60-70 of the enemy (or *Dushman* in Pashtu) into the long low building and were incrementally destroying them *with* fire. But we were not as successful fighting in the south. We had had four killed, and eleven wounded. We had lost two LAVs and witnessed dozens of local nationals killed and wounded in a very large VBSIED[1] attack in the Panjwayi District Centre. Yet, by afternoon those events were behind us. The dead and wounded were evacuated, the LAVs were being recovered, the streets in Panjwayi Centre were being cleaned, and three fresh platoons had arrived – veteran

---

[1] Vehicle-Borne Suicide Improvised Explosive Devices (IED)

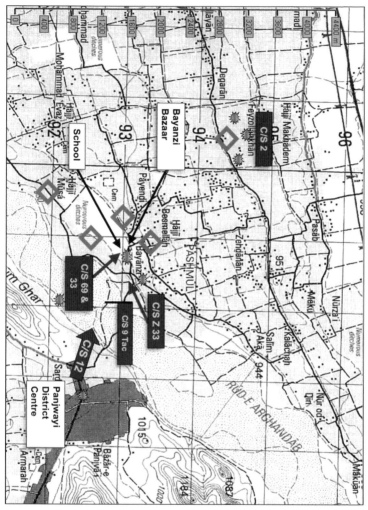

MAP 1: Pashmul, 3 Aug

platoons, each with 4 LAVs and 40 soldiers. Call Sign One-Two
(C/S 12 – which is the radio designation for A Company's 2 Platoon)
had been with us for several hours and was familiar with the ground
and enemy. C/S 13 (A Company's 3 Platoon) had joined us and
was fresh and ready. These troops had traversed this ground before

during the second battle in Pashmul and were battle-hardened. And C/S 31 had arrived – 7 Platoon from Charlie Company – "fighting three-one" I called them, a hard-hitting organization, itching to fight. We still had the bulk of Reconnaissance (Recce) Platoon (C/S 6) and C/S 33 (9 Platoon of C Company), decimated from the fighting that day, but reconstituted and capable of fighting on. I wanted very much to take this force and advance and destroy the enemy at the bazaar in Bayanzi. With these competent and hardened soldiers, together with our supporting artillery, we could do it. More would be killed and wounded, but we would prevail and again drive the *Dushman* from that area. I wanted very badly to do this. I had been in the Arghandab River wadi for twelve hours and was ready to finish what we had started earlier that morning.

Twelve hours before, the picture was different. We had stood in the same place in the wadi in the moments before the sun began to show above the 4000-foot knife-edged ridge just east of us; the Regimental Sergeant-Major (RSM) and I watching Corporals (Cpls) Nic Lewis and Jason Lamont working calmly to revive any sign of life in Cpl Chris Reid. He lay on the stretcher, VSA (Vital Signs Absent). For the hundredth time during this tour I cursed silently while watching and listening intently for signs of a MEDEVAC chopper (medical evacuation helicopter) due any moment on the southern horizon. Once more I felt the deep sense of sadness only known to battlefield commanders who witness firsthand the cost of tactical decisions we have made. This sadness became an unwanted companion. As I helped to carry the limp bodies of Warrant Officer (WO) Shaun Peterson and Reid to the chopper, silently bidding them a soldier's farewell, I felt a now-familiar internal swell of determination to kill the enemy who had done this, and moved onto that task.

Reid's was not the first blood drawn that morning. After a sleepless evening at Patrol Base Wilson our convoy, consisting of C/S 33, Recce Platoon, and my Tactical command group (Call Sign 9er Tac – pronounced "Niner-Tack"), drove the circuitous 40-kilometre route to Panjwayi District Centre arriving there at 4:00 AM. I navigated in the lead vehicle until the district centre, and then during the pre-dawn hour C/S 33 took the lead to assault from southeast to northwest across the Arghandab and breach into the objective area (a bazaar comprised of 8-12 buildings just northwest of the burnt-out white school in Bayanzi, Pashmul). At approximately 4:15 AM, as the four LAVs of C/S 33 quietly and without emitting light snaked out of the wadi and rolled slowly and silently toward the objective, they identified through their thermal sites a group of Taliban in early warning positions astride the axis-of-advance at a range of approximately 150 metres. C/S 33 requested permission to engage and I gave consent; they then hit an unknown number of the enemy with concentrated fire. I watched, 100 metres back, the tracer rounds creating a punctuated arc of flame as the large bullets flew to their mark, exploding on impact and shattering the quiet darkness with the thunderous BOOM-BOOM-BOOM of 25mm cannon fire.

It was in manoeuvring toward these enemy positions after this contact that Reid's LAV was struck by a buried pressure-plate-activated IED (PPIED), fatally wounding him and rendering WO Peterson unconscious. Once they were evacuated I moved forward after daybreak to inspect the initial enemy positions that C/S 33 had cleared. The Taliban fighters had hastily withdrawn leaving rations, weapons, ammunition and intact IEDs, and numerous blood trails. That they had left so much behind indicated the severity of their casualties and their inability to carry everything away. The *Dushman* always policed-up their battlefield immediately, carrying off wounded, dead, and all equipment, before the firing ceased, seldom giving us the pleasure of finding their dead or wounded. I suspect this is something they had learned long ago, perhaps from studying Viet Cong tactics. It was a universal procedure, and highly effective as it frustrated our soldiers, hungry to see the result of our fires.

The enemy had emplaced 5 IEDs along a 100-metre stretch of road coming out of the wadi and up to a short bridge crossing a small canal. We had managed to get one LAV across the bridge before the IED that killed Reid (driving the third LAV) exploded. Every indication gave the impression that more IEDs lay directly ahead in the road on the other side of the bridge leading to the bazaar in Bayanzi, our only axis-of-advance. This was heavily canalized terrain. The thick mud walls on the sides of the narrow roads had been loop-holed so that the enemy could fire upon us from multiple directions without exposing themselves. The numerous irrigation ditches (4-6 feet deep and often covered with grass) wound like First World War trenches between the walled compounds and the fields. The objective area lay across two such ditches, obstacles to our advance that were dominated by walled compounds within small-arms range. It had been three weeks since we had last fought on this ground. We cleared the enemy away from it in early July; but they had returned, and prepared themselves well for this next battle. The thick foliage of fruit orchards, grape fields and tall, lush, hash crops obscured much of our observation toward the objective and due north. But we knew from seeing the evidence in the first positions cleared that the enemy would have prepared defences deep into the objective area. This number of IEDs in such a small space was unprecedented.

In manoeuvring into a position to cover the objective and to provide cover for the recovery of our immobile LAV, another LAV,
E15C under engineer Sergeant (Sgt) Vachon struck an IED, rendering it immobile, and forcing us to once again call in a MEDE-
VAC for three sappers suffering minor wounds. This caused us to
change the mission. We were going to Bayanzi to conduct a Sensi-
tive Site Exploitation (SSE) upon what the locals were saying was a
Taliban transit station. What was to be a clearance of a suspected
Taliban meeting place had now become a large recovery operation in an area dominated by enemy fighting positions. Realizing
this, I conferred with the Recce Platoon Commander (Captain
(Capt) Jon Hamilton) and Sgt Vaughn Ingram – now acting Platoon Commander C/S 33. These were two of the most aggressive
and able combat leaders in the Task Force. Together we inspected
the abandoned enemy fighting positions and discussed options.
I directed them to conduct a dismounted (on foot) clearance of
the area to the north of our damaged LAVs and to be prepared to
accompany the ANP in clearing the school 400m west of our position in order to prevent it being used as a position to fire upon our
recovery operation. This would also have to be done on foot,
without LAVs in intimate support, because it was almost a certainty
that the single narrow road ahead of our lead vehicle was laden
with IEDs and open to fire from multiple walled compounds. There
was no appetite to risk lives and the destruction of more LAVs or
G-Wagons. I abandoned the desire to clear the bazaar in Bayanzi
and focused upon the requirements of recovery.

Changing the tactical mission was a constant in this war. Everything
in Afghanistan submits to incredible friction. All plans change with
the breakdown of one vehicle, the wounding of one soldier. Despite
training and doctrine that stated otherwise, it became my practice in

battle to stop tactical manoeuvring of sub-units in order to extract casualties. Instead of pushing this function back to echelon personnel while commanders carried on with attacks and kept momentum going, the company commanders and I began to engage ourselves personally in casualty evacuations, ensuring that every possible resource was in place to keep soldiers alive and bring medical evacuation forward. Likewise, I was adamant that we would never leave a damaged fighting vehicle on the battlefield, even if it were completely burnt out, as a monument for the *Dushman* to gloat over. So vehicle recovery, like casualty evacuation, often became the mission during operations. One may criticize the inevitable loss of momentum this brought. To this I respond that the destruction of no number of Taliban was so important as the safe evacuation of one Canadian (or Afghan) soldier, and that no number of Taliban killed was equal to the propaganda victory they would have by the abandonment of one of our LAVs on a battlefield and its televised image on the evening CNN Broadcast. The reality of wounding and death changed our notions of the need for tactical momentum in a fight. Commanders became personally involved in evacuation. It became our Number One concern in battle, with positive effect. Soldiers came to understand that if wounded or killed, their recovery from those hellish close-quarters was the first priority of the chain of command, beyond any "prize" of Taliban defeat. We did not have to articulate this, it came naturally in mutual understanding and, I believe, in trust. So, by 9:30 AM on 3 August our assault transformed into MEDEVACs and a recovery operation for two broken LAVs.

At this time we began once again to receive harassing small arms fire. I walked back to the Tactical Command Post (CP) to orchestrate the receipt of recovery assets, low-bed trailers, and Explosive

Ordnance Detachment (EOD) support, and to order forward the reserve Platoon (C/S 12) from Kandahar Airfield (KAF), to direct my
ANP liaison officer to move more ANP forward, to request more attack helicopter (AH) and close air support (CAS), and to once again
call for supporting artillery fire. I began also to monitor and support
B Company's evolving fight north of Pashmul – which was steadily
building into a large entrapment of dozens of Taliban.

It was not until noon that the forward movement of forces had been
completed and the necessary supports were in place. The EOD team
began to sweep the damaged LAV sites and the recovery operation
was awaiting their green light to begin extracting those vehicles, but
this work was increasingly hampered by enemy fire. Things became more complicated as intelligence continued to flow in that our
silent night manoeuvre had surprised the Taliban in that area and
had trapped a Taliban commander in the school just to our west.
I gave the executive order for Recce Platoon Commander (C/S 69)
with C/S 33 and ANP to move forward and clear the white school.
Shortly after closing toward the building the ANP received fire from
the Taliban and immediately fled. As the fire intensified around our
recovery site, I ordered C/S 69 to continue to clear forward. At the
time, the Taliban began to drop mortar rounds onto ANP positions
1800 metres to our southwest.

At 12:30 PM, C/S 69 led a daring and determined assault onto
the school, despite knowing of the overwhelming Taliban superiority in numbers. Capt Jon Hamilton reported by radio that he had
made it to the north end of the white school but that his force was
under intensive enemy small arms fire and rocket-propelled gre-
nade (RPG) fire from several directions. They were caught in the
open with only several low walls for cover. I ordered reinforcements

forward on foot. C/S 12 – just arrived from KAF – dismounted and moved forward with stretchers. Before they could begin to advance, C/S 69's force was hit by even more intensive fire, including a direct hit on their position by an RPG. He reported wounded, including multiple heat casualties. It was 50 degrees Celsius! He then reported multiple VSA, and many WIA, including himself. His transmission was cut off as his radio was hit by fire. Sgt MacDonald charged across an open alley filled with fire to attend his wounded platoon commander and to organize the others to continue to fight. He directed every man to put on a fresh magazine of ammo, seeing that the enemy were closing in upon them. The Taliban desired strongly to secure Canadian soldiers – dead or alive. Even those who were severely wounded manned and fired their weapons in what was a desperate struggle for their lives. One last transmission followed as Capt Hamilton panted into his handset that if we did not get LAVs up there now, they would all die. Every soldier within earshot of a radio speaker heard these transmissions. I did not need the radio to know that things were bad. I could discern from my position 500 metres away the intensity of the enemy's fire as our soldiers fought for survival behind those insufficient walls – pinned down in what was truly a hell. They needed help now.

I had already deliberated upon the implications of losing more LAVs and soldiers to the likely IEDs emplaced between the lead LAV and the school. But the intensity of fire evident just ahead of me, together with the real desperation of that transmission, left us with no options. Drawing attention to the IED threat I asked Master Corporals (MCpl) Parsons and Perry commanding the LAVs from C/S 33 if they thought they could make it to their dismounted soldiers. They said they could. All I was able to offer them after a sad pause was "good luck". That they were already rolling forward indicated that the crew commanders were going to go in anyway, regardless of my decision. A force greater than my authority compelled them forward – pure brotherly commitment to their suffering comrades. Necessity had become the father of courage at all levels. These two leaders – and their crewmembers – displayed courage that has not formally been recognized. Sgt Tower, on foot, had also moved forward into the fight. When he realized that his acting platoon commander and friend (Sgt Ingram) was pinned down with his platoon members, he ran into the fire and – accompanied by two others – courageously managed to traverse the deadly open ground to take command of the remnants of the attacking force and organize their extraction once the LAVs arrived.

I ordered C/S 12 to remount and to follow into the fight, and waited anxiously to see if C/S 33's LAVs got through. Their two LAVs ran a gauntlet of fire and arrived without triggering any IEDs. They rolled up either side of the pinned down infantry, and fired over 400 rounds of ammunition each at the *Dushman* machinegun and RPG positions. Even this was insufficient to win the firefight – over fifty RPGs came their way; but it was enough to slacken enemy fire enough to begin evacuation of the wounded. C/S 12 then rolled into the area of the school and began to suppress the enemy as A Company soldiers began to help pickup the remainder of the wounded C Company men, then the living and the dead. The casualties needed to be collected and sustained until the MEDEVAC helos arrived. The only shade in the entire area was granted by two pieces of modular tentage off the back of a Bison vehicle that was my Tactical Command Post. It was well positioned close to the fighting, yet it protected the MEDEVAC Helicopter Landing Site (HLS) in the wadi. In this position we were under sporadic small arms fire and susceptible to the enemy mortar fire. I directed the casualties to muster at the CP and warned the RSM. It was 52 degrees Celsius in the tent and many of our incoming casualties were from heat exhaustion, men physically unable to move limbs. By 12:45 PM the scene at the baking Tactical Command Post was surreal. I was working three radios, attempting to coordinate AH support, CAS, artillery support, while bringing in MEDEVAC birds for a mass casualty extraction, push for the EOD task to proceed (under fire) and to get the damaged LAVs recovered. The main radio link to the Task Force Tactical Operations Centre in KAF was not working. The main Tactical Satellite radio (TACSAT) was partially functioning. I could transmit on the TACSAT, but not receive their transmissions. Just outside the tent flap on my left side lay three dead Canadians. I did not know it but one of them was Sgt Ingram, unrecognizable to me in death. In the tent I was surrounded by wounded and pushed into the corner by their numbers. Capt Hamilton was there, seriously wounded by shrapnel, as were six others. Several were in battle shock – staring with blank expression at nothing on this plane of existence. Even the men attending them suffered. Cpl Felix had been in the fight and was physically unwounded, but after he had brought his comrades into this piece of shade he just stood there, unblinking at the scene of moaning prostrate soldiers. I quietly promised him that I would get us all out of this situation and told him that I needed him now. He came back instantaneously and proceeded on, with clear professionalism and the competency that I had previously seen in him. Sgt Tower moved through the injured and reported to me. I asked where was Sgt Ingram? "Dead" replied Tower and I realized that one of the bodies I had been looking at was my old Airborne comrade. He had been severely wounded by the RPG blast, yet despite his own wounds he began to apply First Aid to a wounded soldier. He then simply stated that he was slipping away, slumped his head back, and died. Beside Sgt Ingram lay Private (Pte) Kevin Dallaire and Cpl Bryce Keller, who had both died as true soldiers do, one moving forward into enemy fire, the other exposing his body to lethal fire in order to bring his weapon to bear upon the Taliban, not shirking or stopping despite the intense fire and certain fear. I told Tower to give me 100% stocktaking to ensure that no one and nothing important was left behind in the enemy kill zone. He reported back 10 minutes later that all was accounted for, that he had three functioning LAVs and 9 dismounted infantry left in the platoon, enough to take out one or two compounds. Which enemy did I want him to attack, he asked? I felt humoured, humbled, and inspired by his dedication and tenacity. Here was a true fighter. I told him to mind a defensive posture until I sorted out the evacuations and recovery. These proceeded, interrupted by the fire that passed overhead, mortar round impacts too close for comfort, and the largest explosion I have ever seen 800 metres behind us in the Panjwayi District Centre. A vehicle suicide bomber had attacked our recovery convoy, but had been forced to detonate early as he was engaged by the situation-saving actions of Lieutenant (Lt) Doug Thorlakson, who fired a C-6 machinegun burst into the attacking driver as he tried to bear down upon the convoy. The detonation was huge, but because of Thorlakson's actions the bomb exploded too far from our vehicles to damage them or wound our soldiers. Unfortunately innocent Afghan pedestrians were killed in the blast. From our forward position under fire, the explosion and subsequent silence was ominous, adding to the already surreal situation in the CP. The RSM later described the totality of the situation by suggesting it was like having every Performance Objective (PO) Check we had ever encountered in training in twenty years occurs in a single hour.

I knew from the VBSIED that we were enveloped, and that the enemy were coordinating their efforts to trap and annihilate us. At that point we did not have the tactical initiative. It had to be regained, but that would be possible only after the casualty evacuation and recovery were complete, both now jeopardized by increasing enemy fire. We were in danger of becoming pinned down in that wadi, unable to execute any of the evacuations and recovery tasks without abandoning something or someone to the enemy. We fired a danger-close artillery strike as I begged quietly on the silent radio for immediate air support. To my astonishment and joy, within minutes the entire earth shook as a US Air Force B1 Bomber, appearing as if from outer space, over-flew our position at 500 feet in a manoeuvre that I am certain is outside of all regulations pertaining to the employment of these planes. The pilots had heard our distress and decided to add a psychological boost. I cannot adequately describe the impact of receiving air support like this. It is as if in the middle of a lonely fight for life, the hand of a true angel descended to give us decisive help.

With the pass of the B1, followed by French Mirage fighters, the enemy fire thinned, the initiative hung in the balance, and we conducted the MEDEVAC and recovery. This, in retrospect was the hard part. Before the B1 bomber brought the initiative back into balance we had attempted many times to coordinate all the broken parts on the battlefield, while under fire. With the B1 Bomber pass, I quickly delegated the entire mass MEDEVAC to the RSM (even though this was something that I normally was personally involved in as well). I delegated our immediate defence to Sgt Tower and Second-Lieutenant (2Lt) Ben Richards (C/S 12), I pushed G19 to fire danger-close, and I delegated to the superb Capt Brian Fleming (12 RBC Surveillance Troop Commander) the task of handling the VBIED in Panjwayi District Centre. I then directed my battle captain, Capt Kevin Barry, to move forward to the EOD and recovery site (150 metres away) and begin to make progress on these two critical things (stalled for 3 hours). Kevin was one of the finest young officers I knew, commissioned from the ranks, tough, reliable, and practical of mind. Working with C/S 12 and the recovery and EOD Non-Commissioned Officers (NCOs), he quickly executed a controlled EOD explosion and jerry-rigged the LAVs so that they could be pulled back to the hard stand at Panjwayi District Centre by double chains to two harnessed LAVs. Kevin's actions affirmed a long-standing principle that I reiterated throughout the TF; experienced senior NCOs recover vehicles, young officer do security. Kevin being both in knowledge and talent handled this dangerous and complex task beautifully. If the Army has not yet done so, this scenario must be replicated in training – multiple vehicle recovery under fire (both direct and indirect) with heavy threat of unexploded subsidiary IEDs under the vehicles. It doesn't get much more harrowing.

With these critical tasks done, and with fresh platoons now available, I faced that hard decision. We had regained the initiative, with freedom to act as we wished. Up until this point in the tour, we would not have even hesitated. We would have attacked. Our emotions, our desire for retribution, our innate drive to defeat the *Dushman* this day, and every day, was compelling me to organize an attack now. But chewing yet another cigar, I had to admit that personal impulses were clouding the reality of this. One fact of that reality was that we did not have a company commander present to carry on this fight, and if I fulfilled that function, no one could coordinate between this fight and B Company's further north, or A Company's or C Company's in their disparate Areas of

Operation (AOs) far to the north and east. Earlier that day I had violently come to realize the mistake I had made by not having either Major (Maj) Kirk Gallinger or Maj Bill Fletcher forward with me. They were both far away, in Showali-Kot and Spin Boldak, engaged in their own skirmishes. Another factor was that we had no Afghan National Army (ANA) attached to our force. At this point of tour ANA had become a scarce commodity, and we seemed to have to work more often without them than with them. Lack of ANA support had plagued us for four months, and despite frequent promises by a dozen good-intentioned generals, nothing changed. The only consistent "Afghan face" on our operations was that of the Taliban.

Without ANA it was impossible to produce more than a temporary effect upon this enemy. We could fight that night, and would succeed once again in driving the enemy from Bayanzi by morning. We would have more men killed in the process, but we would prevail; yet, to what effect? We would have to withdraw the next day without having positioned any ANA or ANP forces on that ground to sustain security there. The *Dushman* would return within three days.

Finally, we were now no longer under Operation Enduring Freedom, but under an ISAF (International Security Assistance Force) mandate; and that day it became clear the difference in cultures that this transfer brought. Under Operation Enduring Freedom there was a prevailing philosophy of "mission command", with echelons of headquarters pushing resources to the commander in the fight, and asking him what more he needed. There was never second-guessing or micro-management of the battalion's battles. Under ISAF the philosophy was reverting to one of tight control of everything by general officers many hundreds of kilometres away.

The fighting of 3rd August was done without the benefit of intimate support fires from the Canadian Artillery; it was the first battle of our tour where combined-arms effects were prohibited by over-restrictive fire control procedures. My passion to kill the *Dushman* that night was considerably offset by my equally emotional need to go back the KAF and sort out a better system for fighting; and to convince the Brigade that this enemy in Zharie and Panjwayi meant business and could only be destroyed by a large concerted effort. That night the concept of Operation Medusa was born, and the next day we would begin the very serious preparations for a large-scale battle on this ground, one that would take the majority effort for our replacement force (TF 3-06) when they arrived, one that was to have lasting effect. The Canadian mission had just entered a new stage of deliberate containment of the Taliban's efforts to seize Kandahar City.

How did this come to pass? How did we get to a point where Kandahar City was so threatened, and what lessons can we learn from that journey? These I will attempt to answer in the following narrative outlining the efforts of TF Orion to beat the *Dushman* between January and August of 2006. It is written to capture the valuable lessons that we learned by way of great pain.

Introduction

Between January and August 2006, TF Orion operated throughout southern Afghanistan with good success. This tour of operations was marked from all others of the past 50 years by the sustained combat endured by the soldiers. TF Orion had over 100 contacts with the *Dushman* and 50 of these involved intensive firefights, complex manoeuvre, and the use of artillery fire and support aircraft. These engagements took place across the map of Regional Command South (RC-S), in three provinces, as the TF clocked 1,700,000 kilometres of driving; on one operation conducting 600 kilometres of combined-arms manoeuvre. At one point the TF was fighting 240 kilometres from our second echelon in KAF. In all this the Maintenance Platoon kept our Vehicle Off Road (VOR) Rate at an astonishing average of 10.5%, and Transport and Supply Platoons (and all those superb persons involved in the incredible feat of logistics that spanned half the globe) ensured that we never ran short of vehicles, or the necessary supplies of parts, ammunition, water, fuel, or food. Despite the extremely harsh conditions, morale remained high, discipline infractions were rare, and in all of this fighting no civilian casualties were incurred, and only one minor concussion was sustained as a result of friendly force fire. These actions took from the enemy almost 500 of his fighters, and cost Canada the lives of 14 brave men and women. Their sacrifice contributed to the success of the TF in setting the conditions for NATO assumption of responsibility for command in Afghanistan, and prevented Kandahar City from falling into Taliban hands during the contested summer of 2006, elevating the credibility of the Canadian Forces and the nation to its highest levels in generations. By all counts, this was a successful mission.

What follows is an account of this mission from the eyes of the TF Orion commanding officer. It recounts what I consider to be key events and actions of historical interest. As such, I hope to educate the reader on what must become part of Canadian military history, because the actions and sacrifices of our soldiers have earned an honoured place in that field. Also, and perhaps of equal interest, it is a personal reflection of challenges in command, why I made certain decisions and how I dealt with stress. I write this with the simple aim to help those who are preparing to carry on this fight, in what is truly "The Long War".

There are three command imperatives frequently reinforced throughout this account. Firstly, *a commander must comprehend the nature of the war that he finds himself in, and avoid attempting to turn the reality into something that it is not.*[2] The fight in Kandahar is a one of counter-insurgency, not a peacekeeping operation, not a counter-terrorist campaign (although that is also occurring in the special operations domain), and it is not a battle against a constituted opponent army. A commander must comprehend that in this counter-insurgency fight, no purely military victory is possible. It does not matter how many *Dushman* we kill in fierce pitched battles, because this is not a conventional war against an enemy army. It does not matter how many "high-value targets" (HVT) are eliminated, because our conventional forces are not in a counter-terrorist campaign. It is wrong to simply rely upon presence patrols to show the flag as a deterrent, for this is not peacekeeping. We must conduct instead continuous company and battalion offensive combat and non-combat operations

---

[2]   This of course is from Carl von Clausewitz, *On War,* ed. And trans. By Michael Howard and Peter Paret, (Princeton: Princeton University Press, 1976), 88-89.

to keep the enemy off balance. The best we can hope for is that our tactical military actions continuously increase Afghan confidence and keep the enemy disrupted so that the operational initiative rides with us, buying time for the eventual growth and maturity of the Afghan National Security Forces (ANSF), and for governance and reconstruction reforms to gain traction. Winning confidence and maintaining the operational initiative were not abstract ideas to us in TF Orion. They became real entities, tangible commodities that we could sense movement in, ebbing and flowing based upon our actions and the effects of our information and psychological operations. We did everything – combat and non-combat – to keep the enemy guessing and to reduce his options. We applied a lot of thinking into staying completely dynamic and unpatterned, and doing everything we could to diminish the enemy's status. Our fight became more of an intellectual struggle to out-think and outwit the enemy and keep local support than it was a physical contest to kill or capture the *Dushman*. It was a violent dance. Combat was conducted as much for moral as for physical effect. It was a command imperative that I understood counter-insurgency well, and did not try to see this fight in terms of other types of conflict.

From our experience emerged the second imperative: *that a commander recognize that in war the human being, and human personality, is everything.* War remains today, as it was when Agamemnon met Priam, a violent clash of independent human wills. Under the baking Afghan sun we rediscovered that the first determinants in war are human. In combat the power of personality, intellect and intuition, determination, and trust, outweigh the power of technology, and everything else. At the moment of close-quarter combat between these opposing wills, when extreme violence, casualties, heat, thirst, uncertainty, and pressure, tactical solutions and success come from the human heart and head. Amongst the rank and file there are a small minority of natural fighters whose tenacity and courage work to solve problems and defeat an opponent, the others just observe and follow these few, out of respect and trust. Around these few fighters emerge small combat groups whose love for each other is the first and last determinant in combat. No technology, no type of organization, no political ideal will supplant this commitment and the bonds it forms between primary group members (in groups of 4-10 strong). Therefore, it is the establishment of primary group cohesion that a commander must attempt to establish prior to combat, and it is the maintenance of human cohesion that he must protect in battle. This foundation, not technology, is the key to tactical success.

The third imperative is: *that a battle commander cultivate a sense of moral purpose and not be given to careerist and managerial leadership practices.* The Canadian soldier is a combat soldier and requires from our NCOs and officers combat leadership, not garrison management techniques. Combat is a highly personal experience, in which the cultural predisposition of a soldier is translated into action. Combat also provides opportunity for the individual to throw off the trappings of civilization and temporarily submit to primeval instincts. A combat commander must observe sub-unit sub-cultural predispositions and guard against excess based upon primeval impulses. Through continuous moral reasoning and action he must personify the centre point of moral well-being in a unit. If well led, the Canadian soldier has the ability to move through the experience of brutal combat and acquit him-or-herself well, not becoming ruled by primitive discharge, but achieving missions without recrimination. Our soldiers differ from European counterparts in that they fight more readily, and with greater tenacity and more aggression than most NATO comrades, yet they remain more disciplined than less professional soldiers. This is the legacy the modern Canadian soldier has inherited from countless anonymous professional officers, warrant officers and NCOs who strove for the past two generations to keep alive the fighting ethos and the standards of good discipline in our military; and TF Orion was greatly indebted to this countless many for their unrecognized effort to keep professionalism alive and careerism at bay. What our soldiers need most is leadership that understands this inheritance; personal, hands-on, and trusting leadership that stays present in times of danger, understands the psychological needs of the soldier, shares risk with them, and solves for them those problems that they themselves cannot solve. Our combat soldiers need combat leadership. This is prerequisite to the establishment of vertical cohesion within the Canadian Forces, from the Chief of Defence Staff (CDS) to the private, embracing the natural trusts within primary social groups and expanding upon this to connect the primary groups to determined and professional NCOs, WOs and officers who remain present with these groups, in order to enforce discipline over emotion in situations where fear, anger, and remorse are natural, and in order to maintain the greater credibility of the Canadian Forces. Soldiers caught in situations beyond the scope of their experience and problem-solving skill will look to a commander in a manner that begs: "what the hell do we do now sir?" To meet the demand of this moment we must inculcate a value system within our leaders that demands the highest standards of professional competence, moral reasoning and judgement over the careerist impulses that are currently pervasive, courage, fierce determination, and control of emotions. This last trait is paramount. The Canadian Forces in war require combat leaders who possess a moral robustness of spirit not common to other professions.

I learned these imperatives while in command of TF Orion, the name we gave to the 1st Battalion Princess Patricia's Canadian Light Infantry (1 PPCLI) Battle Group (BG) and its attachments. This comprised three rifle companies or "manoeuvre sub-units" (A and C Companies 1 PPCLI and B Company 2 PPCLI) each with over 120 infantry soldiers equipped with LAVs, G-Wagons, and Nyalas; an Artillery Battery (A Battery 1st Royal Canadian Horse Artillery) equipped the newly acquired M777 155 millimetre Howitzer; an Engineer Squadron (11 Field Squadron of 1st Canadian Engineer Regiment); a Headquarters Company comprising a Reconnaissance Platoon and sniper group from 1 PPCLI and a Surveillance Troop from 12e Régiment Blindé du Canada in Valcartier, Québec (equipped with Coyote surveillance vehicles), and a Military Police Platoon from 1st Military Police (MP) Company in Edmonton; a Tactical Unmanned Aerial Vehicle (TUAV) troop, a Health Services Support (HSS) company of 60 medical personnel; a Forward Support Group (FSG) consisting of maintenance, logistic and transport personnel; and the Kandahar Provincial Reconstruction Team (PRT) consisting of military personnel and representatives from Department of Foreign Affairs and International Trade (DFAIT), Canadian International Development Agency (CIDA), the Royal Canadian Mounted Police (RCMP) and other police agencies, Corrections Canada, and the United States Agency for International Development (US AID).

I chose Orion to give everyone in this uncommon grouping of soldiers, sailors, airmen and airwomen a common identifier, something that might help them bond together more easily. TF Orion was created in September 2005 in Wainwright, at the beginning of pre-deployment training for our mission to Afghanistan. I had been in command of 1 PPCLI for 12 months. We had been warned of our mission to Afghanistan in October of 2004, and were told by General (Gen) Rick Hillier in March 2005 that we would go to Kandahar under US-led Operation Enduring Freedom (OEF). So by September my RSM, Chief Warrant Officer (CWO) Randy Northrup, and I had created a fairly cohesive battalion team that was focusing upon the upcoming mission. We needed then to expand the team to include our BG and other attachments. We did this by co-locating all of our people in one bivouac, by decentralizing combat support assets and embedding them within combat sub-units, by providing training scenarios that concentrated on establishing broad trust in each arm and corps represented in the task force – mainly through extensive live-fire training – and by forcing people away from sub-unit identifiers (flags and colours) toward acceptance of a common – neutral – identifying symbol. I chose Orion from the constellation – representing the mythical Greek hunter of mountain beasts – that blessed Afghan skies, so that our soldiers might look up and, seeing it, feel part of a larger entity, enduring and meaningful. I used this symbol deliberately to help create cohesion within this unconventional grouping. It is in the creation and maintenance of cohesion that trust becomes meaningful beyond the boundaries of the individual soldiers, and links small groups to a larger whole. These trusts became more pronounced during the intense close-quarter battles that marked our collective experience. Battles, for example, such as we faced on August 3rd in the area south of Pashmul. But there were many other actions before that fight, in all corners of Kandahar province. I want to recount the most important of these actions and elaborate upon the command imperatives listed above. But first, I need to tell you about the situation in Kandahar, and about our mission.

Situation — Ground

The Reg Desert stretches across the southern half of Kandahar province, containing large wind-formed sand dunes blown over a hard-baked crust of compacted sand and rock. The northern edge of the desert ends abruptly at the Dowrey River which winds east to west across the province before joining the Tarnak and Arghandab Rivers in Panjwayi. The confluence of these rivers in central Kandahar explains why throughout the centuries multiple tribal groups settled here. To the east lies Arghistan and Maruf, a hash of wadis, ridges, valleys and mountains, uniformly brown and dusty. To the north of the city there is a 15-20 kilometre belt of barren volcanic rock and sediment, black in colour, which indicates a steady rise in elevation toward substantial mountains of Ghorak, Showali-Kot and Mienishin. These are forbidding mountains surrounded by a morass of ridges and deep V-shaped valleys, completely covered by forests of boulders of all sizes (there are no woods here), scattered in endless piles on every slope and crest. Often single trees stand atop of ridgelines, silhouetted against the mountain sky, giving soldiers landmarks with such names as "Lone Tree" or "the Joshua Tree". The valleys contain green orchards and fields, even though the soil is still baked dry and brown. When TF Orion began operations here in February, all intelligence told us that the *Dushman* would repeat his perennial habit of massing forces in the mountains of Showali-Kot and attempt ambush and IED attacks toward Kandahar City. But when we eventually found him massing, it was in central Kandahar; in the complex of green and walls of Panjwayi and southern Zharie, where we fought on August 3rd.

The map reveals that here there is a large right angle triangle of green cultivated land, 40 kilometres wide on its eastern side

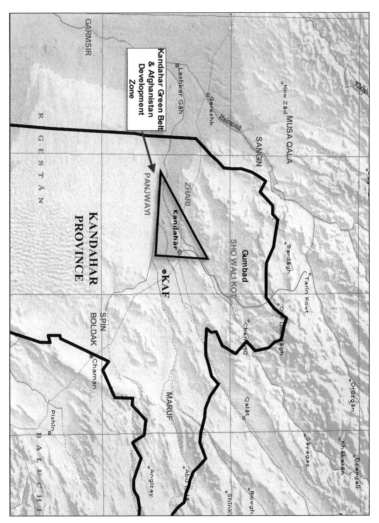

Map 2: Northern Kandahar

(incorporating Arghandab, Kandahar City, KAF and Tarnak) and fifty kilometres long on its south side – ending at a sharp vertex in the west at the juncture of the Arghandab and Dowrey rivers, where the green belt whittles down to a few kilometres of cultivation. This triangular green zone is covered by a veritable maze of ditches and walls encircling fields, farms and villages.

The villages consist of individual family compounds, each with three to five structures and enclosed by an eight-foot wall of dense mud and brick (impenetrable to most of our weapons). Similar walls connect the family compounds to one another, the intervening spaces containing crops or an orchard. The "streets" that run through villages are little more than expanded paths or, at best, narrow roads, framed by tall thick walls on both sides, broken only by doors or gates into the compounds. While each village has one or two main arteries twisting and turning through it, there were innumerable alleys running willy-nilly between compound walls and fields that made soldiers feel like lab rats moving through a maze. The main streets do not run straight but meander, varying in width and direction in ways that make it impossible, without accurate aerial photographs (maps will not do) to know where the street will turn next and which direction it will leave the village. Often the roads run over canals or ditches that are difficult for our wide and heavy vehicles to cross. Many have concrete culverts and bridges just wide enough for us, but often the culverts are made of mere thatched wooden poles (branches really) reinforced with mud and supported by some clever-placed rocks. Quite often too, the roads are almost completely covered over by foliage of lush trees, the most difficult to us being the mulberry tree, with thick branches which – when the turrets of our LAVs hit them – damaged some of our equipment, and worse still, dropped hundreds of mulberries into our crew compartments – staining everything brownish-red, a colour very similar to the stains of dried blood.

PHOTO 1: Arial Photo of Pashmul

Each village complex was connected to other villages by narrow roads, and between each there were large orchards and fields of grain (or poppy depending on whether it were first or second harvest), hash plants, melons or grapes. The grain and poppy crops would only grow several feet tall in the spring harvest, while the hash crops in the fall would grow incredibly dense and up to eight feet tall, making each field a forest, well-suited for hiding. Although the hash fields were imposing, the grape fields were the most astounding. Each consisted of dozens of rows of raised furrows made of hard-baked clay, two and half feet high, and the grape vines would grow out of the tops of these furrows, thick and tall, so that the troughs in between the furrows were covered over by grape vines, making these superb places to hide men and weapons. The orchards were equally lush and shady. Thick baked-brown walls and winding ditches compounded all these fields and orchards. Irrigation here was essential to life. Ditches were four to six feet deep and wide enough for men to walk single file in, fully armed. They were often covered from aerial view by shady trees or long grasses, making them preferred transit corridors for the *Dushman*. Many of the ditches connected to deep wells, which were cavernous holes in the ground that lacked any fencing or surrounding walls, so that soldiers walking on patrol at night could, and did, in one pace leave solid earth and step onto nothing but air, and fall a dozen feet into a well of cold muddy water. Some isolated farms existed between villages, often elaborate compounds containing the houses of landowners made affluent by poppy. In many fields stood grape-drying huts; buildings sixty feet long, 15 feet wide and 20 feet high, with a doorway in one end. The walls of these "huts" were four feet thick at their base and contained three rows of ventilation holes, slits really, six inches wide and a foot high, that allowed the inside of the hut to breath. The roof of each hut consisted of a very thin layer of thatched grass, easily penetrated by 60mm mortar rounds. These huts were used to hang grapes until they dried into raisins, and to shelter Taliban groups during the heat of mid-day.

The inhabitants of most villages were from a single tribe, or a mix of allied tribes. A village could be as small as four family groups, or as big as four hundred family groups. Regardless of size, an "elder", who would usually be the first villager to approach our patrols after we arrived, spoke for each village. In bigger villages, several elders might appear; indicating that governance there was through a council of elders. In many villages we would begin sitting with an elder and commence an impromptu "shura" (meeting) and quickly be joined by a dozen or more other men, their arrival and the sitting position (relative to the first elder) would belie their status in the community. Women were never present.

Seldom were women ever seen outside of compounds. One advantage of the LAV was that it allowed us to see over compound walls, and so to glimpse into life behind the walls. Afghanistan has a large female population, unknown to the travellers who ride in cars or on foot. These women live behind walls and seldom leave unless in the company of a man, and decked out in full burqa. When we passed their compounds and could see inside, viewing women without headscarves, their reaction was mixed. Some – the elderly – quickly went inside. Many stopped and looked directly at us, unveiled and unafraid. Some – obviously with men absent – smiled openly and even waved. It was difficult to see these women and not feel immense sadness, the feeling akin to what you might feel at a zoo when seeing a caged tiger pacing, except tenfold sadder. Each village was run by ancient code and practice that regulated everything in village society, within which women – especially girls at puberty – were property; a commodity used in trade to solidify tribal connection, to pay off debts of honour, and that assured growth of the family unit.

DANCING WITH THE *DUSHMAN*

Social control, emanating from the elders, determined everything;
which little girl would receive a new dress, how much water each
farmer would draw. The water that flowed into each irrigation
ditch was controlled and apportioned out to farmers according to
need and status, so that around the clock one could observe men
in the fields damming a ditch and opening a dam for his ration of
water, measured by hour or minutes of flow. The mosque kept time.
Sometimes the loudspeaker wired to the mosque roof revealed the
only electricity evident in the village. Five times a day the quiet of
the village would be broken by a telling electric crack as the loudspeaker received power, the cue that a call to prayer would follow.
The mosques were evident to us by these loudspeakers, the schools
and clinics were also obvious, they were the newer western style
buildings that were burnt out and pillaged, clear indicators of the
continued presence and influence of the Taliban.

The enemy decided to fight us in Panjwayi and Zharie, in the
green zone, amidst the incredibly dense and superbly defensible
terrain there. It allowed them sanctuary. Here they could live off the
land, finding plenty of food locally, and having easy access to the
well-stocked markets of Kandahar city. Here they could move and
conduct raids and ambushes well concealed by the vegetation. This
area provided plenty of water and shade. It contained a critical mass
of tribal groups traditionally supportive of certain Taliban leaders
(mostly ex-Mujahadin leaders), and in those villages where tribal
affiliation did not prevail, there was seldom a large enough male
population of a single tribe to challenge the presence of an armed
Taliban group. The green zone had good lines of communication
to the mountain sanctuaries to the north, to the Pakistani border to
the east and south (mainly through the river wadi networks of the
Dowrey, and Tarnak rivers, but also by trails across the Reg Desert).

The area was linked to the larger and more secure Taliban sanctuaries of the Helmand river valley through Maywand District only 30 kilometres to the west. The enemy chose his ground well.

Situation – Enemy

In Kandahar province in January 2006 there were an estimated 200 indigenous Taliban fighters. By this I mean 200 armed and dedicated men who lived in small groups around the province and whose life's purpose was jihad against the Afghan Government and Coalition Forces. At any time, one small group could be joined by hundreds of other fighters of two varieties; local farmers who for money or by coercion would fight alongside Taliban groups who entered their territory for whatever expedient purpose – usually to secure poppy and hash harvests or because of familial debt or tribal affiliation to a Taliban leader; and groups coming from Pakistan comprising a mix of hardcore "foreign fighters" (Chechens, Uzbeks, Arabs, or Kashmiri insurgents), and partially trained jihadists from the refugee camps and madrassas who were moved to parts of Afghanistan to bolster the ranks of local Taliban forces. In May 2006, we could sense a build up in the numbers of fighters in the Zharie/Panjwayi areas through an infusion of all three types; indigenous Talibs, conscripted farmers, and groups of foreign fighters and jihadists. By June, a conservative estimate would put the figure at 400 fighters in Zharie/Panjwayi alone, ready to begin operating inside Kandahar City.

Regardless of their make-up, insurgent groups increasingly came under direction of superior Taliban commanders. During fire-fights we treated all these fighters the same – as *Dushman* – and attempted to kill or capture them without discrimination. But in our Information Operations campaign (using the Psychological Operations (PSYOP)) detachment on the battlefield, the company leaders sitting in shura with the locals, or in our PSYOP products and media events) we attempted to force divisions between the various components of the fighting groups. It became an explicit goal to drive wedges between the local conscripted fighters and the hard-core foreigners and to persuade the locals to stop fighting, while encouraging the others to accept the Government's amnesty program or be continually hunted by us.

The primary group for the insurgent consisted of five fighters, with one RPG gunner, one PKM machine gunner, each with an assistant, and a commander. This group constituted the basic fire and manoeuvre unit on the battlefield, and was the perfect size to travel from place to place, unarmed, without drawing attention, using a single car or several motorbikes. They seldom fought in-dependently. Rather, three or four other groups would combine at a pre-designated location, recover cached weapons and supplies and, under a single dominant commander, plan and conduct raids and ambushes. ICOM transmitters and cellphones constituted the primary means of communications used to coordinate movement of these groups, their re-supply, their battlefield manoeuvre and fire, and their casualty evacuation. There was one ICOM for each 5 or 10 man-group, and one cellphone for each amalgam of 20-40 fight-ers. The fighters were armed with traditional insurgent small arms – AK 47s and AK 74s, PKM machine guns, RPGs, and on occa-sion 82 mm mortars, light recoilless anti-tank rifles, and a seemingly endless supply of IED-making equipment (although in reality the material needed for IEDs was becoming scarcer).

The hardcore Taliban fighters were physically fit, tough, experi-enced, and ideologically inclined to sustain discipline in combat. They were extremely loyal to their commander and would fight hard to secure his safety. Conscripted jihadists were less inclined to

PHOTO 2: Taliban Fighters
From US Army threat briefing presentation given to author, August 2005

sustain discipline in firefights, and while they followed the lead of the seasoned fighters obediently, the accuracy and effectiveness of their fire was limited. Locally recruited fighters displayed the least battlefield discipline and would often leave the fight after the first exchange of fire; they seemed to fight long enough to demonstrate that they had fulfilled an agreed-upon degree of support for the Taliban, but not long enough to be at risk.

All these fighters had similar tactics, techniques and procedures (TTPs). Planning was important to all *Dushman* groups, whatever their mission. They would not merely reconnoitre the terrain to be fought over – they studied it, becoming familiar with every possible infiltration and extraction route, all ditches and fighting positions, possible IED sites, etc. They were assisted in this by history. Many of the areas where we fought were exactly the same as those contested during the Soviet-Afghan War. Indeed some of the senior Taliban fighters had twenty years before personally used the ambush positions along Highway 1, between Howz-e-Madad and Ashoqah, to attack Soviet and Afghan Government convoys.

Once a plan was made, the execution was swift, involving night movement on foot or by cars and motorbikes to the ambush or raid site. Occupation was made with extreme discipline to allow surprise to be complete. All *Dushman* actions began with as intense an initiation of small arms and RPG fire as possible. At night PKM would initiate with tracer fire, giving the RPG gunner something to aim at. Alternately, during the planning stage the *Dushman* would reconnoitre in daylight and place two aiming sticks in front of firing positions so that upon occupation at night the RPG gunners would simply align the tube between the two sticks keeping it at the same height as the top of the sticks to ensure that elevation was correct. Some of the enemy did use night vision equipment and laser range-finders. Initiation of fire was signalled by both PKM weapons fire and by ICOM communication. In ambushes there were always redundant early warning stations along avenues of approach to the ambush site; the *Dushman* never mistook our columns for the civilian traffic that passed before or after our vehicles.

The enemy would fire with intensity for several minutes, almost always inaccurately and with limited effect. If he outnumbered us, the *Dushman* would attempt to pin us down in his kill zones, and outflank us. Only if he was certain that he had us separated and outnumbered would he attempt to swarm in to kill or capture a Canadian – a highly coveted prize. Otherwise, he remained at a distance of 100 metres or more and applied his fire in hopes of producing casualties. When he sensed that we were ready to bring in artillery fire or AH or CAS, he withdrew to another ambush position astride what he believed to be our line of advance and would wait patiently there, holding his fire until we once again came into view. If he continued to fight after we began to apply supporting fires, we knew that he was having a hard time extracting his casualties, or that he was fighting to gain time for the withdrawal of a senior leader, his money, or his opium. If these were not an issue, the enemy would withdraw completely from the area once he was worn down by the fighting.

The *Dushman* studied us and adapted quickly to attempt to surprise us. They would observe the commencement of our operations (normally cordon and searches in specific villages) and forecast our lines of advance and rate of movement. They often spent their day preparing an ambush in a position that we would close upon just before last light, when they would hit us, always from two sides (if not three).[3]

The *Dushman* always attempted to use firing positions that had obstacles (canals, walls, grape furrows, hash fields) between themselves and their targets, in order to prevent us from closing quickly upon them. This bought them time. Whenever we cleared through their fighting positions, often within minutes of the end of

---

[3]   The close and complex nature of the terrain in Zharie/Panjwayi (and along the Helmand River), combined with our terribly under-strength platoons and companies (the formal leave program – HLTA – drew our numbers down by 1/3) made it impossible to prevent the enemy from using this tactic; unless we massed the whole task force onto a small area, as we did in July 2006.

firefights, we found them cleaned, with little remaining evidence except cartridge casings and blood trails. This phenomenon was repeated so often that it came to be expected, and we had to be satisfied finding only body parts or blood trails, and were surprised when we actually found dead or wounded left on the positions. Casualty evacuation was reinforced by the Pashtun cultural practice of burying dead by nightfall of the day of death. The enemy always planned for withdrawal and extraction of casualties before he commenced fighting, and executed the withdrawal with great speed. We knew from ICOM chatter and local informants that they had pre-designated vehicle pickup points and secret holding areas for casualties, as well as rudimentary field hospitals in specific compounds in Panjwayi and Zharie. Their ability to cleanup their battlefield was disconcerting to us, who wanted to see the tangible effects of our fire.

The enemy's command structure was fairly rigid at the top, with the supreme Taliban council undisputedly in charge (four members of whom were from Panjwayi). Below that there was much more dynamic politics at play. Several senior field commanders (who could call upon 100 fighters or more) were well established in their districts and unchallenged. However, if they did not fight up to the expectation of the supreme council members they would be berated and another senior leader might be brought into the district to kick start attacks against us. Likewise, proven junior commanders with their five to twenty-man groups would be moved around frequently, giving support of local commanders who had demonstrated willingness, and success in fighting.

The 200 fighters that faced TF Orion in January 2006 tripled in number by June, and massed in the green zone of

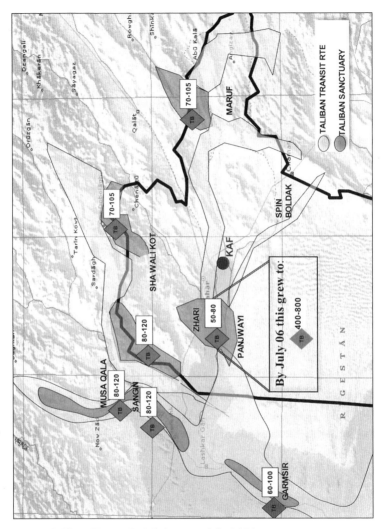

MAP 3: Taliban Threat Model, January-July 2006

Zharie/Panjwayi. In the Helmand River Valley to the west there were another 400-600 fighters, spread from south of Lashkar Gah north through Gereshk, Heyderabad, Sangin, Musa Qala, and to the Kajaki Dam. Additional fighters had come from Pakistan via the Bahram Cha pass into southern Helmand, then north along the river to the sanctuaries at Sangin or east to Panjwayi. Alternate routes took them through the Reg Desert on shifting roads suitable for light vehicles (cars and pickup trucks). It was not difficult to move such fighters around during this period. The harvest season brought the migration of a large labour force, moving from farm to farm, creating conditions in which it was easy to mask the movement of fighters amidst the larger movement of farm hands. By July it became evident that insurgent and local fighters operating in Helmand and Kandahar numbered in the thousands.

After weeks of fighting in May and June, and because of multiple reports from local Afghans that stated such, we were convinced that the Taliban were massing in Panjwayi to establish a permanent base of operations there, with a view to attacking Kandahar City. Speculation arose in May 2006 about the plausibility of a large-scale "spectacular" attack upon the city, which if prosecuted, would result in a bloodbath there, and an irreversible loss of confidence in local national and international resolve. We had witnessed how the situation was being portrayed in the press and we understood the effectiveness of Taliban propaganda. It was not out of the question that the Taliban were considering creating effects similar to the Tet Offensive of 1968, designed to shatter national will in Canada and Europe and arresting momentum toward the NATO takeover of southern Afghanistan. When this idea was expressed to senior Coalition commanders and staffs it was dismissed as reactionary, and the Zharie-Panjwayi area received limited attention by our intelligence organizations. TF Orion, however, continued to make it our main effort.

Situation – Friendly Forces

The indigenous counterpoint to the Taliban was the ANA, the ANP, the presidential-appointed Governor, and the elected Provincial Councils. There was a severe shortage of ANA soldiers in southern Afghanistan in 2006. Those that were stationed in the south had been partnered with Coalition special forces (SF) and used to guard their forward operating bases (FOBs) and to support the SF operations. The remainder suffered from high tempo, as they were piecemealed out in small groups (15-40 strong) to provide "the Afghan Face" to Coalition operations all over RC-S. Constant change and depleting numbers made it very difficult for these forces to work above the platoon level. On operations they proved to be very brave during combat, loyal to those willing to suffer alongside them, quick on their feet, but simple in tactics. During the course of our fighting together we had to teach them to not charge the enemy immediately upon contact, but to let our LAV and artillery to first "win the firefight". Each ANA detachment came with a Coalition Embedded Training Team (ETT), a dozen coalition officers and soldiers that live, train, and administer an Afghan unit. We were fortunate to have very good ETTs partnered with us, the most noteworthy being a French Marine special forces team of great experience and wisdom, and a US Army Reserve team under Maj Blake Settle, whose physical courage and compassion for his charges created strong cohesion. We – Canadians, ANA, and ETTs – enjoyed working together, and it was common in firefights to see all three uniforms firing and moving side-by-side toward the enemy.

To reinforce their confidence, we integrated the ANA commanders into our planning and established a combined BG tactical command post where ANA and ANP commanders and staff could live and work during operations. I also personally promised the ANA three things: continuous escort of their flimsy pickup truck transport by our LAVs whenever we were operating together; coverage of all their tactical movements by Canadian artillery fire, and the exact same medical evacuation and treatment that was accorded to Canadians. We also promised to help with their strained logistic system, frequently giving them rations and money for fresh rations (purchased from locals). In exchange we were given promises that these soldiers would die for us; a promise they fulfilled on five occasions – unfortunately. I loved working with these troops. I hated that Task Force Orion was never afforded a formal standing partnership with any particular ANA unit. Instead we were forced to practice continuous adhocry, short-notice tasking, and change; all of which made it needlessly harder for Canadian, Afghan, American, and French soldiers. Quite often we had to operate without ANA, which made it difficult to find the enemy, as the ANA were superb at communicating with locals (who universally respected them) and at collecting intelligence.

The local's respect for the ANA was contrary to their feelings for the ANP. The ANP were Afghan, yes, but they were in no way "National" in character nor were they remotely identifiable as "Police". They ranged in quality from tough and loyal groups of fighters, to highly corrupted thugs with uniforms, whose only credentials were their affiliation to a district or provincial leader, to gun-packing youths who were relatives of these men, neither trained, nor caring. They often preyed upon villagers, especially those from different tribes. Some ANP could fight for short periods, but we quickly learned (on April 14 – when many died in stupid attacks against Taliban forces) that they were best at roadblocks and checkpoints. The exception in all this was Capt Massoud, a one of a kind. Massoud commanded the Governor's own quick-reaction police, largely made up of fighters loyal to the Governor (Massoud himself had been employed by the Governor for 17 years). Massoud was in his late thirties, an ex-member of the Northern Alliance, exceptionally well spoken in English, very intelligent, and passionate in his hatred of the Taliban. He wrote everything down, rare in Afghan culture, and could organize complex tasks. I always asked for his support and spent countless days in the field living and fighting alongside this inspiring man. I trusted very few other ANP officers, and firmly believed that some of the others had played a role in targeting my command vehicle for suicide attacks in June. I practiced a careful intelligence exchange with them, and although we gave the ANP advanced warning of operations, we never allowed them to know exactly when, where, or how we were about to launch attacks. I sometimes used the ANP in deception operations, telling certain suspect officers wrong dates and targets with full expectation that this information would be quickly passed to the local Taliban.

PHOTO 3: Captain Massoud (ANP)   Courtesy of Author

Massoud was the single most important source of intelligence

The Governor of Kandahar held my respect in that he was a strong man who had great potential. Also English-speaking and clever, he held influence with, and was a loyal man of, the Karzai family. He had been the Governor of Ghazni before, but his natural inclination was for national security work and he fancied himself the next Minister of the Interior. Because of this he was inclined to ignore developmental work and we had to persuade him to govern over reconstruction and development initiatives. He would have rather played *Uber*-cop. He disliked the ANA because they were not responsive to his orders (being a national force under the Minister of Defence), and he considered that all police in the province worked directly for him, even though constitutionally they worked for the Minister of the Interior. He was both lauded and rebuked for charging to Sangin in January when there were clashes there between Taliban and Helmand ANP. He liked to go to fights, carrying a gun and dragging the media with him. This was his desired image, the strongman – a fighter-Governor.

On 14 April, we permanently changed that image for him. A spoiled attack and an ANP friendly-fire debacle which killed several of their best fighters had made the Governor very angry. I saw him standing with his gun in the fading light of Howz-e-Madad after the failed attack. He blamed Coalition forces for being too slow to arrive and too cautious to get into the fight. He declared that from that point onward he would command all fighting in Kandahar province. I had just arrived from east Sangsar village where my crew and I had found and personally patched-up a number of wounded ANP and called in the MEDEVAC for their evacuation to KAF. Four of us had used all of our personal first aid equipment (including seven tourniquets) on these ANP casualties, and carried their bleeding light-weight bodies to the helicopters. One of these was a well-known, one-legged, ex-mujahadin hero called Kater Jan, whom I drank tea with occasionally, and wounded with him was his 14-year-old nephew, out with uncle on apprenticeship combat training. That the boy wore an ANP uniform bothered me considerably. While doing this gruesome work, I came to piece together the events of the day and was angered and saddened that they had lost so many just because they would not wait for our arrival. They had only one tactic, to charge at anything that fired at them, assuming that personal courage was more powerful than the flying bullet. They would not wait for us to coordinate LAV and support fires, and this impatience had cost them. The Governor and I had a heated exchange regarding the complexity of modern warfare, the authority of military command, and the civil role of governors. Thereafter we established a system wherein I would plan operations with ANA and ANP representatives and back-brief the Governor on the plan before commencing. To help us all, I reinforced the Provincial Coordination Centre, a combined Canadian/ANA/ANP operations centre inside the Governor's compound, where combined planning occurred, and where the Governor could access liaison officers at any time of the day or night. As well, we established the aforementioned joint command post upon the initiation of each battle, providing the official venue for all combined tactical decision-making between ANA, ANP and ourselves. The Governor was never invited there.

TF Orion assumed responsibility for Kandahar from the US Army's Task Force Gun Devil, a composite battalion consisting of an Artillery unit headquarters with infantry, anti-tank, and artillery sub-units. While not doctrinally sound, this grouping became highly effective under the superb leadership of their command team, LCol Bertram Ges and Command Sergeant-Major Willey. We received from them an excellent handover – which included several skirmishes with Taliban forces before assuming full control of the area on 19 February. For the next two weeks we worked under command of the US Brigade HQ TF Bayonet, an extremely efficient organization with an outstanding combat commander – Colonel (Col) Owens. However, this warrior wanted very much that the Canadians demonstrate to him their willingness and ability to fight and I was pressured constantly and intensely in mid-February to assume several tactical missions that I did not think we were ready to conduct. It took a week of discussions with Col Owens for him to realize the strategic significance of our first missions and to understand how important it was to have initial mission success – both for the task force and for the nation. I realized during this that the US Army is not yet familiar with coalition warfare and its political dynamics.

In early March, Bayonet was replaced by TF Aegis, the Canadian-led multi-national brigade headquarters, consisting primarily of Canadian, American, British, Australian and Dutch staff officers whose role it was to prepare RC-S to be subsumed under NATO/ISAF control (from US-led Coalition control) by 1st August.

Mission

Our mission was stated thus: "TF ORION will assist Afghans in the establishment of good governance, security and stability, and reconstruction in the province of Kandahar during Operation ARCHER (Rotation 1) in order to help extend the legitimacy and credibility of the Government of Afghanistan throughout the Islamic Republic of Afghanistan and at the same time help to establish conditions necessary for NATO Stage 3 expansion."

Ours was a transition mission. Canada had accepted the lead role in RC-S for the period that would see the transformation of mandates from the OEF to the NATO-led ISAF. ISAF had expanded in 2004 from its presence in Kabul to take charge of northern Afghanistan (Stage I) and then western Afghanistan (Stage 2) in 2005. Stage 3 expansion foresaw ISAF taking over southern Afghanistan – the most difficult transition given the volatile nature of the south.

The US demanded that NATO-ISAF demonstrate combat capability in RC-S as a pre-condition to transfer to ISAF control. This was problematic because the vast majority of NATO nations refused or were reluctant to assume responsibility for areas where fighting occurred regularly. But if this pre-condition of demonstrated combat effectiveness was met, and Stage 3 could occur, it was thought that Stage 4 (ISAF assumption of eastern Afghanistan) could come into effect rapidly, unifying all of Afghanistan under one military Headquarters. No other nation had volunteered to see Stage 3 transition through. It was impossible for the US to do this effectively. The British felt that domestic political factors would preclude them from leading in RC-S so soon after they were seen as following

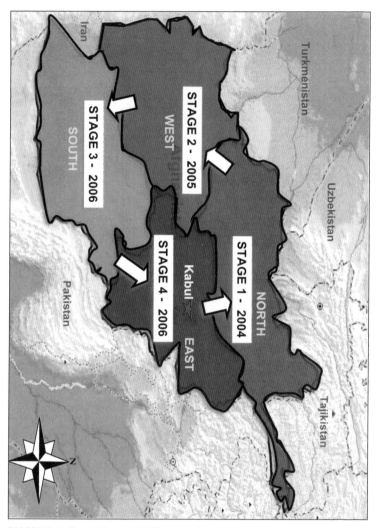

DIAGRAM 1: Transition to NATO Control

obediently into Iraq. The Dutch had refused to work under OEF. Other continental European countries balked at the idea. Canada accepted the leadership role for both OEF and NATO at this critical juncture. The vehicle to deliver this transition was a Canadian led multi-national brigade headquarters led by Canadian Brigadier-General (BGen) Fraser, and the combat-capable TF Orion.

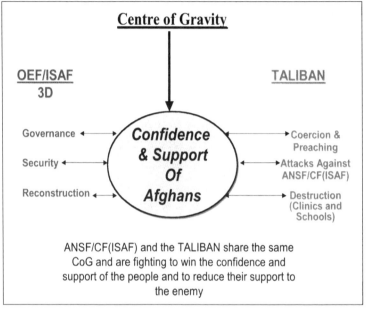

DIAGRAM 2: Centre of Gravity

TF Orion's tasks were multifarious, divided into three broad categories: governance, security, and reconstruction. These became our lines of operation (broad sets of connected objectives and tasks that contribute to the elimination of the key problems or obstacles to our mission). The key problem in my mind was the winning and maintenance of the confidence of the people (who were at the same time subjected to considerable pressure by the Taliban to support their cause). In this sense, the struggle in Kandahar was essentially a clash of human will, between forces loyal to the Government of Afghanistan (GOA) and those opposing this authority, with the people of Kandahar in the middle, being pulled, enticed, persuaded and coerced to choose sides. In traditional Afghan fashion the people will side with whomever they believe will win. We needed to be deemed as the probable winners. The confidence and support of the people was essential to allowing freedom of movement and action; for both the Taliban and us. We both relied upon the same source for such freedoms and support. The people constituted a common "centre of gravity" that we wrestled over. When you come to understand the conflict in these terms, you can easily see the importance of trust. Establishing trusting relationships with local authorities and with the people was essential to swaying the centre of gravity to our side. This model became the basis for a common understanding of the nature of counter-insurgency operations in Kandahar. We began to assess our tactical actions against how they would increase or diminish confidence. I show this model as an example of the first Command Imperative; with it we clearly articulated a counter-insurgency mentality, not conventional warfare and not counter-terrorism, both types of conflict that do not put the people at the centre of the struggle. It was important for me in all subsequent decision-making that I understood our tactical actions in terms of ultimate purposes – the winning and maintenance of local confidence, and measured our effectiveness against this litmus test. Occupying ground and pursuing favourable "body-counts" were meaningless.

As an operating concept I intended that the 1 PPCLI BG become an extension of the PRT so that I could coordinate and synchronize all TF tasks in a unified effort under one chain of command. This centralized control was to be exercised in a manner responsive to desires of Afghan authorities and their people. We used the combined Afghan/Coalition Provincial Coordination Centre at the Governor's Palace to help build the capacity of provincial civil, police, and army leaders in managing security. Likewise, I wanted the PRT to operate downtown in order to work with the provincial staff to coordinate international agency reconstruction efforts and to assist in the functioning of the Provincial Development Committee (PDC). This would give the provincial leadership powerful centralized organizations that could assist them in exercising their authority while building their capacity to govern effectively. All of our efforts would focus upon creation and development of a Afghan Development Zone (ADZ) that incorporated the triangular area around Kandahar City and foresaw massive coordinated initiatives for enhanced security, governance, and development in this small area to create a "shining example" of political, economic and social success that other districts would quickly want to emulate by evicting Taliban forces and transforming from poppy crop to legitimate crop economies.

The Afghan Development Zone concept originated in Gen Hillier's ISAF Headquarters during his tenure in command of ISAF in 2004. It was the result of a strategic assessment that was subsequently handed to Lieutenant-General Richards and his staff to commence implementation during his tenure as ISAF Commander in 2006. The concept was transferred and fully developed by a group of Canadian staff officers situated in various headquarters (prime amongst these was LCol Paul Duff at the Allied Rapid Reaction Corps Headquarters and Col Mike Capstick – Commander of Canada's Strategic Advisory Team in Kabul 2005-2006), who ensured continuity of this counterinsurgency methodology during periods of change in commanders. I was personally involved in the formulation of the initial ADZ concept in 2004 and 2005. It was a wonderful thing to be a commander charged with the first phases of the implementation of this strategic concept, and marked how well Canada was progressing in the Afghanistan mission.

While command of TF Orion (BG and PRT) was centralized and responsive to the provincial authorities, the execution of the governance, security and reconstruction tasks was very decentralized. We pushed elements of the manoeuvre sub-units out into independent sub-unit Areas of Operations (AOs), located in places that would allow daily work with Afghan National Security Forces and district leaders to improve governance, security and socio-economic conditions in key districts of the province. We organized for decentralized operations, evolving to the point where within a platoon there were multiple attachments embedded (engineers, medics, and Civil-Military Cooperation (CIMIC) – personnel). These "platoon groups" became the agile multi-functional instruments of the counter-insurgency fight.

To enhance provincial and district governance, the TF elements were to engage village, district, and provincial leaders to convince them to implement GOA initiatives. I wanted every platoon-group patrol to stop in villages and conduct local shuras (meetings) to hear-out the people and to encourage the elders to engage district leaders. The patrols reported results to the sub-unit commanders, who in turn engaged district leaders to properly represent the villages to their provincial leaders. The PRT Commander and myself engaged the governor and his staff and provincial council to hear representation from the districts. TF patrols were also tasked with reporting village and district reconstruction requirements to the PRT and to monitor the progress of reconstruction projects in rural areas. The PRT led in assisting provincial leaders in establishing reconstruction priorities, building their capacity to manage reconstruction projects in a legitimate manner. At the same time TF elements were to operate with and train the ANSF throughout the province in order to create ANA capacity to conduct independent counter-insurgency operations, and to build ANP capacity to enforce the rule of law.

While we were committed to this 3-dimensional (3D) approach, two things combined to focus our efforts upon the security line of operation. The first was a loss of momentum in PRT activity resulting from the tragic death of diplomat Glynn Barry in January and the long review of the PRT by Foreign Affairs Canada (FAC) and CIDA that followed, with a cessation in their funding to the PRT for six months. The second was a steady increase in Taliban activity until June when it became obvious that a full-blown Taliban offensive was underway in southern Afghanistan that threatened our ability to achieve NATO Stage 3 and to establish the ADZ. Our efforts were then drawn more and more into responding to this threat by executing a long series of sub-unit and BG operations to find, fix, and finish the enemy.

Concept of Operations

Finding the Enemy

In pre-deployment training scenarios it was impressed upon TF Orion leaders that we would have access to incredible intelligence resources that would enable us to execute deliberate plans against pinpoint targets with less risk. The assumptions behind this assertion were formulated from the experiences of Canadians in the Balkans and in Kabul, neither of which was a counter-insurgency fight across an expanded battlefield. The assumptions were true for counter-terrorist operations in confined areas (such as Kabul), but not for the situation we found ourselves in. The reality for TF Orion was that very limited higher Intelligence/Surveillance/Reconnaissance (ISR) resources were available to us, and none of it directly. Our own integral assets were very limited in capability and capacity. At best we would be given grid references where there had been a communications hit on a suspected enemy leader, but seldom details of who and what. This lack of detailed intelligence, combined with the big blunt nature of our LAV-based capability, made it impossible to plan and execute rapid deliberate precision operations from KAF. After attempting it several times, I even began to question the purpose of these strikes. A temporary hit against a Taliban leader would do little to win the confidence of the locals.

The counter-insurgency nature of the fight in Kandahar demanded a much more dynamic, flexible, and responsive operational concept. Therefore, we began to deploy forward into company and platoon areas of operations and we lived amidst the locals, in the face of the enemy, out of the back of the LAVs. This put us closer to the enemy and if we received "actionable intelligence", it shortened our response times and increased our chances of achieving surprise. It also gave us access to local intelligence. Like beat cops, we became aware of the environment and were able to sense measures of local confidence and the swing of operational momentum.

PHOTO 4: Living Outside-the-Wire   Courtesy of Major Steve Gallagher
(author stagging-on with coffee and smoke while crew sleeps)

Intuition and trust became central in our efforts to find Taliban forces. Over time we began to decipher which Afghan information sources were reliable (and which were not) and to trust our instinct, regardless of whether or not they were confirmed by higher intelligence capabilities. I began to trust the subordinate commanders to act − or not − upon this local HUMINT (Human Intelligence).

Given the lack of intelligence about the enemy, there were few specific missions given to TF Orion by the brigade during our first four months, so it was up to us to establish tempo and task, and these became almost entirely dependent upon the personalities of the commanders, and it is here that I can introduce the second command imperative: the power of personality in war. All of the leaders in TF Orion could have very easily hunkered down into localized routines in relatively safe areas, following a pattern of "framework patrolling" and by this be seen as "busy", when in fact we would achieve little (except to surrender the initiative and set ourselves up for IED attacks). Instead, I forced myself and encouraged – and trusted – the company commanders to be perpetually proactive in hunting the enemy, forcing everyone to live "outside the wire" and to continuously manoeuvre and to engage locals. This was difficult for everyone, especially after casualties were incurred, when there was always a natural tendency to adopt caution and reduce tempo. It was at these times especially that I trusted the subordinate commanders to demonstrate an aggressive spirit and maintain operational initiative through offensive action. Not all people are equal in this regard and the Army must learn that robustness and determination are not nice-to-have qualities in manoeuvre commanders; they are core qualities, and we must work hard to select the few who have the tenacity to sustain a high level of resolve in the face of danger.

Our living out-of-the-wire allowed TF Orion to transfer from operation to operation in efforts to find the *Dushman*: conducting 27 such operations between March and August.

We commenced BG operations in early March, and that month brought our first serious casualties. I recall returning from Showali-kot on March 3rd, when the news came across the radio of the terrible vehicle accident that claimed the lives of Cpl James Davis and (belatedly) MCpl Timothy Wilson. They had attempted to veer out of the way of an Afghan vehicle that had cut them off in Kandahar

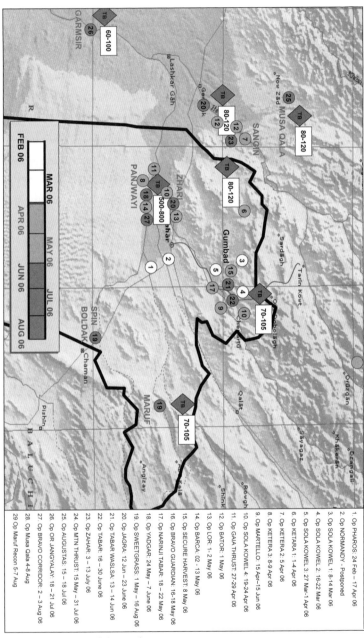

MAP 4: Summary of Operations

1. Op PHAROS: 24 Feb – 17 Apr 06
2. Op NORMANDY - Postponed
3. Op SOLA KOWEL 1: 8–14 Mar 06
4. Op SOLA KOWEL 2: 16–22 Mar 06
5. Op SOLA KOWEL 3: 27 Mar–1 Apr 06
6. Op KETARA 1: 1–4 Apr 06
7. Op KETARA 2: 5 Apr 06
8. Op KETERA 3: 8–9 Apr 06
9. Op MARTELLO: 15 Apr–15 Jun 06
10. Op SOLA KOWEL 4: 19–24 Apr 06
11. Op GAIA THRUST: 27–29 Apr 06
12. Op BATOR: 1 May 06
13. Op LOR: 1–2 May 06
14. Op BARCA: 02 – 13 May 06
15. Op SECURE HARVEST: 8 May 06
16. Op NARINJI TABAR: 18 – 22 May 06
17. Op YADGAR: 18 – 22 May 06
18. Op BRAVO GUARDIAN: 16-18 May 06
19. Op SWEETGRASS: 1 May – 16 Aug 06
20. Op JAGRA: 12 Jun – 23 June 06
21. Op TABAR WASLSA: 13 – 14 Jun 06
22. Op TABAR: 16 – 30 June 06
23. Op ZAHAR: 3 – 13 July 06
24. Op MTN THRUST: 15 May – 31 Jul 06
25. Op AUGUSTAS: 15 – 18 Jul 06
26. Op OR JANGYALAY: 18 – 21 Jul 06
27. Op BRAVO CORRIDOR: 2 – 3 Aug 06
28. Op Musa Qala 4-8 Aug
29. Op Maruf Recon 5-7 Aug

58

city traffic when their LAV rolled. We had not even said goodbye
to these men when my own vehicle was hit in a suicide IED attack
on March 4th, gravely wounding MCpl Mike Loewen, the alternate
crew commander. The crew acted superbly. The attack occurred
just seven kilometres from KAF, and MCpl Loewen received first
aid and was placed into a Bison for transport back to the airfield.
However, the Bison caught fire enroute, and MCpl Loewen had to
be hoisted unceremoniously out of the top hatch of the Bison and
placed upon the roof of a G-Wagon for open transport back to the
hospital, soldiers on either side of him strapping him down as the
G-wagon used best speed to ensure that Loewen made it to the sur-
gery table in time to save his damaged arm. The following day in
Showali-kot Capt Trevor Greene was seriously wounded in an axe
attack during a routine – seemingly benign – village shura. He was a
superb CIMIC officer, dedicating his work to help the people of this
remote region. I was at the hospital when they brought his bleeding
body in on US Army helicopter, and found myself having to harden
my sentiments in the wake of this brutal and unprecedented attack.
We were beginning to have engagements with the enemy on Highway 4 between KAF and Kandahar City where they chose to ambush us, and in Showali-kot, where we had occupied the Gumbad
Platoon House. These first casualties produced a toughening of our
souls, but also gave us increased confidence in the capabilities of our
vehicles and in casualty evacuation chain.

The casualty evacuation chain, the medical resources in the Task
Force (60 superb medics in the HSS coy), the MEDEVAC birds of
Task Forces STORM and NIGHTHAWK, the world-class Role 3
Hospital on KAF, the unequalled C-17 MEDEVAC flights from
KAF to Landstuhl Regional Medical Centre in Germany, and
outstanding Canadian MEDEVAC channels back to Canada,

granted the soldier of TF Orion the very best medical support system ever in place in a combat operation. As a commander I took time to become very familiar with each component of this, to organize medical SITREPs about our casualties in KAF and Germany, and to educate all commanders on the processes of MEDEVAC, so that when they first occurred we had more confidence. A commander must never underestimate the morale-enhancing effect of knowledge of the MEDEVAC system. Soldiers wounded in battle do not want to leave their comrades to move back into the unknown. Soldiers who watch their buddies disappear from the fight long to hear news about their condition. It is a command responsibility to push knowledge over fear and keep everyone informed. In my case, I attempted to have the soldiers identify the MEDEVAC birds, the Role 3, and the Landstuhl Hospital as direct extensions from Task Force Orion, and not some uncaring "other".

In early March, B Company and Recce Platoon focused on the threat on Highway 4, and A Company and C Company looked to the Showali-kot and Mienishin Districts. These were critical areas. Highway 4 was our lifeline between the PRT and KAF. Showali-Kot and Mienishin were astride the brand new Kandahar to Tarin Kot road, which was also to be the vital lifeline for the Dutch forces scheduled to arrive in June and July for duty in Uruzgun province. To pacify this area we carried on the occupation of the Gumbad Platoon house in the picturesque Gumbad Valley approximately 8 kilometres west of the Tarin Kot Road. Task Force Gun Devil had established this Platoon House and found that it had severely disrupted Taliban activity in the area. It was located in the midst of a series of villages that had been used by the Taliban as transit areas and for periodic concentration of forces. A portion of the population were sympathetic to the Taliban, the remainder could not offer resistance. In March 2005, TF Gun Devil soldiers had discovered groups of 40-60 armed Taliban walking in daylight around this area, coercing the locals and comfortable in the protection provided by the isolation of this mountainous district. Gun Devil fought hard to change that, and by the time we took over from them in February 2006, no longer could the Taliban move in daylight with impunity. Their operations became covert; group movement only occurred in darkness; night letters were their means of coercion; and only unarmed movement by individuals occurred in daylight (except in the remote mountains of Mienishin where Recce Platoon periodically encountered small armed groups in daylight).

To challenge our sustained presence in the north, the Taliban used IEDs on the limited number of trails that gave us access to Gumbad. To counter this, all the A Company platoons conducted aggressive patrolling, and on three occasions were able to foil IED attacks by capturing and wounding several IED cell members. A Company also conducted multiple operations to cordon and search the compounds of known Taliban leaders; on one occasion accomplishing a 28 kilometre company dismounted night patrol to attempt the capture of a senior Taliban commander, only to narrowly miss him. Throughout February and on into April and May, there were repeated threats of attacks upon the Gumbad Platoon house. Only once was this attempted – a small scale RPG attack that triggered a large-scale response by fire and manoeuvre by 2 Platoon. This occurred in early February, coincidentally happening at the same time as a combined, US/Canadian practice artillery shoot, occurring just 10 kilometres away. LCol Bert Ges and I were able to turn the practice shoot into a responsive combined fire mission in support of 2 platoon. It became apparent from our intelligence sources that the actions taken by 2 Platoon (under Capt John Croucher) on that occasion, coupled with the subsequent aggressive posture of A Company – kept the enemy physically and morally off balance and incapable of concentrating to attack Gumbad.[4]

We stayed in the Gumbad Platoon House on the naïve prospect of overseeing the completion of a government sub-district building in Gumbad, where district officials and ANP would be located. The construction itself was going well, under our permanent security presence, but in negotiation with the government and ANP, we were having no luck in finding personnel brave enough to commit to living and working in Gumbad. Despite this reluctance, the longer that A Company stayed in Gumbad the more effect they had on winning confidence amongst the locals. More and more information came in regarding Taliban movements and intentions. More and more local reconstruction projects were started.

However, we could not sustain this effort. The Gumbad Platoon House was at the end of 5-hour cross-country journey through remote desert and mountainous terrain. Moving personnel and supplies to Gumbad was very difficult and dangerous. We needed to rotate personnel in and out once every 14-20 days, but re-supply requirements and the need to extract personnel going on leave (HLTA) meant that we were forced to traverse the route to Gumbad several times a week. We were denied our requests to

---

[4]   In fact, I once received in March a gist of a conversation occurring between Taliban leaders where the senior was berating the junior commander for not attacking us, asking: "where are they, which villages?" "Every village" was the answer; "How often?" was the next question: "Everyday" came the response: "What about the mountains?" was the final question: "Yes the mountains too...I can see them onto top of one in front of me now" said the frustrated subordinate.

have this re-supply and the rotations of personnel conducted by helicopter, leaving ground re-supply our only option. This cost us dearly. We sustained 10 severely wounded (MCpl Demopoulus, Sgt Charette, Cpl Hand, Capt John Croucher, Cpl Barker, Cpl Williams, Cpl Lindsey, Cpl Levesque, Capt Larose and Cpl Elrick) and 5 vehicles destroyed to IED attack; and on 22 April, 4 good men died when their G-Wagon ran over a quadruple stack of anti-tank mines (Cpl Matthew Dinning, Bombardier (Bdr) Myles Mansell, Cpl Randy Payne, and Lt William Turner). Weighing these losses against our operational gains was no easy thing. It kept me awake.

Even though Gumbad was unsustainable without helicopter support, we were determined not to give up Showali-kot. Therefore, very early in the tour I decided to move our permanent presence from the remote Gumbad valley to the newly paved Tarin Kot Road. A base here gave us the advantage of relatively easy re-supply along a hardtop route (alleviating the IED threat), while at the same time giving greater security to eventual Dutch movement on the single artery between Kandahar Airfield and their new base in Tarin Kot. It also bolstered confidence amongst local people who could see the obvious economic and social benefit of the road but who were still under Taliban influence. This base would sever a traditional Taliban movement corridor comprised of a ten kilometre-wide band of mountains running east-west that was bisected by the Tarin Kot Road. In the middle of this movement corridor was the village of Elbak, long known for its Taliban sympathies and home to one of several key leaders. We decided to build the forward operating base on the hills overlooking Elbak, in an attempt to disrupt the Taliban transit while achieving those other effects. We commenced building in April and by June we opened the large and dominating Forward Operating Base (FOB) Martello. The effect upon the Taliban was significant. They were denied a traditional sanctuary and their perennial transit route. Their inability to stop our construction produced infighting between their leaders, with several senior leaders continuously ordering futile assaults against the FOB, while junior commanders (who would have to conduct the attacks) continued to refuse. Meanwhile, the enhancement of security provided by FOB Martello allowed the Dutch to move into Uruzgun without sustaining one casualty. This had tremendous effect on the achievement of Stage 3, which was predicated upon the British and Dutch occupying bases in Helmand and Uruzgan. Also, local confidence rose. Markets began to grow in the villages along the road and employment opportunities increased. With the arrival of bus and taxis services, people began to gain access to health care for the first time, and schooling opportunities could also be considered. The Taliban had not abandoned this part of Showalikot and Mienishin; but they were careful not to make the people choose between sides, so their activity remained very low-level and their influence was in stasis.

To ensure that the enemy did not seize the initiative and – with the arrival of good weather – concentrate forces against us, we conducted large-scale manoeuvres across northern Kandahar province. We began with Operation Sola Kowel (peace-maker), which saw the manoeuvring of 7 platoons throughout the Gumbad and Kundulen Valley network, in an effort to reach all villages and to introduce the idea of enhanced governance and reconstruction while at the same time demonstrating our strength. These multiple company group movements throughout the area, and the many dozens of *shura* conducted, helped us gain good knowledge of the land and its demographics. Throughout the two-week operation we were frequently given intelligence of pending enemy attacks. These grew in size and portent. During a single night in Gumbad, I was awoken three times to be told that the enemy was massing in the mountains above us, using cave complexes and preparing for attacks, first with 300 fighters, then with 500 fighters, then with 700 fighters. The next morning I issued orders to move six platoons on foot into the mountains above Gumbad – in what we called the "BellyButton feature"– to conduct detailed reconnaissance of all the peaks and valleys and to look for this reported massing of enemy. We started up the mountains the following morning and spent 48 hours kicking stones and looking for caves. We found none. There were several boulder shelters and karizs (subterranean irrigation canals) in the BellyButton where Taliban groups could hide for a short period– but not live in. These were not in use. Locals had no knowledge of Taliban massing in the mountains. So we returned to our vehicles safer in the knowledge of misreporting. We were convinced instead that Taliban fighters were living and moving in the villages, supported by local sympathizers, and not hiding out in caves. We began to discover that the dynamic was always the same. A group of 5-10 fighters would arrive in a village to stay with a relative or friend. The villagers were told to support them with food. Their presence served to intimidate the locals who would not attempt to fight or challenge them for fear of harsh retribution. Only in a small number of villages did we find locals willing to stand up to Taliban attempting to stay in their midst. These were places where there was no tribal affiliation to Taliban leaders and where strong village leadership and the possession of weapons by village males constituted a potential armed counter to Taliban intrusion. The *Dushman* avoided these villages. We also learned from this operation that we had to mass a considerable number of soldiers to properly encircle and search an Afghan village. One company containing two small platoons and some ANA were not sufficient. Rather, we began to plan and execute operations that saw two or three manoeuvre forces moving in darkness to descend upon a village from different directions, cutting off the escape routes. At dawn we would enter and through "soft knock" methods (literally knocking on people's doors and politely asking to search their property) attempt to identify Taliban fighters hiding amongst the locals. Seldom would locals divulge this information if the Taliban or their sympathizers were within earshot. Often we found that lone farmers in the fields would speak more willingly, as would children who would freely provide our ANA soldiers any information they asked for.

Our manoeuvres in Sola Kowel demonstrated to the enemy the incredible agility of TF Orion. Our vehicles had penetrated the most remote villages, our artillery could range into any district in northern Kandahar province, and our soldiers could separate from the vehicles and scale mountains of any height, without restriction. We fired multiple artillery "show-of-force" fire missions to demonstrate the capability of our artillery. We did the same with the LAVs, firing the 25mm Cannon up the side of mountains to achieve plunging fire onto the mountain peaks at ranges of 4 kilometres. Throughout these shows, we continually listened for enemy ICOM chatter and broadcast our own PSYOP messages to him, sometimes taunting the *Dushman* to come and fight us, using manly bravado and personal challenges (naming the Taliban leader) to invoke responses. This made the Taliban very angry and increased their chatter. Our intelligence informed us that these demonstrations of capability in aggressive offensive operations had completely disrupted Taliban designs in Showali-kot. We subsequently repeated this type of manoeuvre in Operations Jagra and Tabar in Khakrez and Mienishin districts. We utilized an effective combination of LAV manoeuvre, dismounted patrols over the mountains, helicopter insertion, artillery fire, and sustainment convoys to show the enemy our considerable combat power. Whenever we started these operations our movements generated a high volume of enemy communications traffic that showed that they were confused about our intentions, nervous about our power, and extremely angry that we were thwarting their own plans.

Our capabilities were best demonstrated in an operation on 24 June targeting the village of Chenartu in Mienishin. Previous special operations attempts against Chenartu had failed, on one occasion with the loss of a helicopter. Our operation began with Recce Platoon conducting a long range infiltration – first feinting a patrol into the North East of Mienishin, then at night doubling back to approach Chenartu from the North East using small remote mountain roads suitable only for the LUVW. Simultaneously that night two LAV companies with engineers infiltrated (with no light emissions) to block off Chenartu from the South. When Recce and the LAV companies were in place we sealed off the North and West by inserting two platoons (including mortars and ANA) by helicopter at first light. A Battery provided fire support from 20 kilometres away. TUAV gave me details of possible enemy movements during our infiltrations. Our surveillance troop secured the lines of communication (LOCs) of the LAV companies. While the enemy chose not to engage us and never revealed any weapons, we concluded the cordon and searches quickly without contact. What marked this operation for me was how it demonstrated the superb range of capability and agility of TF Orion. This was a textbook operation, multi-faceted, and demonstrated the incredible agility and adaptiveness of TF Orion. No single British or US unit could achieve this same compilation of airmobile light force, patrol-vehicle force and LAV force capabilities, all coming together with combined effect upon the same objective. We were wonderfully flexible in how we could plan and execute operations with this composition. I firmly believe that every deployed Canadian task force in the future should have this same capability. Every garrison Canadian infantry battalion should have the capability of two LAV companies (with the LAV crews being trained and administered under Combat support company); three rifle companies capable of falling onto the LAVs, being airmobile, or operating dismounted; a large Recce platoon in light patrol vehicles; and mortars. This is what we used with superb effect in June, July, and August, and it is what right looks like.

While the operations only resulted in minor skirmishes, they were very successful in creating the conditions for progress of FOB Martello, to producing changes along the Tarin Kot Road, and in giving the Dutch the needed security to gain lodgement in Uruzgun without setback. These operations, together with the continued presence and work of A Coy in Showali-kot and Mienishin contributed, in large part, to the creation of favourable conditions for NATO Stage 3 to occur.

Some might argue that the effects of such operations are unclear and short term, and such criticism might be true if we were fighting a conventional war to seize terrain, or a counter-terrorist fight to kill bad-guys. But we were engaged in a different type of conflict. The effects we produced were far more profound than we could appreciate at the time. Canadian activities in these northern Kandahar districts seized the initiative from the enemy and impressed upon him the strength of our fighting force, and the futility of attempting to fight us in mountainous terrain. This effect was not lost upon the locals. They respected our strength; but they also came to respect our discipline and compassion. When we first rolled into villages in

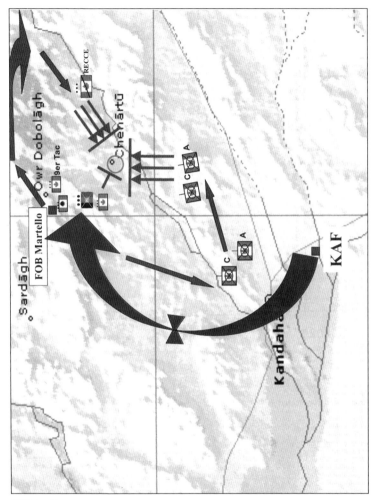

MAP 5: Chenartu

armoured columns and wearing Starship Trooper garb, the locals were afraid. When we then took helmets off and sat to drink tea and talk governance and reconstruction, they were surprised. When we remained for weeks alongside their villages and never abused them, they were grateful. We were clean and disciplined and not given to extreme action by losses to our ranks. The locals, who had for three decades been victimized by bearded thugs with guns – militias, ANP, Taliban – came to respect our professionalism.

Finding the Enemy – Operation Ketara: Demonstrating Operational Reach

In March 2006, 7 Platoon of C Company (Call Sign 31) assumed the role of RC-S Quick Reaction Force (QRF). This force came under command of Capt Graham Smith (my Headquarters Company Commander) who had a small C2 element (JTAC, communicators and medical personnel) that would deal with coordinating fire support, re-supply, casualty-evacuation and communications while 7 Platoon under Capt Hugh Atwell, fought close-quarter battle. This QRF had undergone extensive training and rehearsed deployment across RC-S on several occasions. During the late afternoon of 28 March they received orders to deploy forward to FOB Wolf, just south of Sangin on a high plateau on the east bank of the Helmand River between Kajakis Dam and the town of Gereshk. Four days prior to this the US Special Forces A-Team in FOB Wolf had attempted to attack the compound of a prominent Taliban Commander, only to be hammered hard by many dozen Taliban fighters and receiving US and ANA fatalities. They managed to extract themselves by extensive use of Joint Direct Attack Munitions (JDAM) and had since been holding up in FOB Wolf. The *Dushman* then planned a comprehensive attack upon the FOB and our intelligence indicated that this would occur any time in late March. An ANA reinforcement was sent to the FOB on March 28th; however it was ambushed enroute and sustained 8 killed and multiple wounded before they limped into the FOB. In an effort to pre-empt a large-scale Taliban attack, C/S 31 was inserted by helicopter to the FOB after dark.

I received news at 0300 the next morning that FOB Wolf had been attacked and that there was one Canadian KIA and 3 WIA inbound. I went to the Tactical Operations Centre (TOC) and the Brigade CP and then to the hospital to witness the offloading of our wounded. The serious cases, WO Brodeur, and Cpl Wanvig were run in on stretchers accompanied by two of the fiercest beasts I have ever seen; US Combat Medics from what I believe to be their Delta Force. These individuals had massive builds, burnt faces, long shaggy hair and beards that reminded me of ZZ-Top. I could tell by the equipment they wore and the professional demeanour that they had been through this many times before. I thanked them for bringing my boys out, they replied that they were proud of the conduct of the Canadians.

As these two stretcher cases were pushed into the ward, out of the darkness came a lone figure, walking from the helipad carrying extra weapons and kit. It was Cpl Lynch, a quiet and steady soldier who I had spoken with only once before. Upon seeing him I assumed he had been sent to accompany these wounded. It was only when he sat in the triage room and began to remove a bandage on his leg that I realized that he too had been hit. He scoffed. It was a bullet graze and he stated his complete satisfaction with the Israeli Bandage that he had applied. I was very impressed with his calmness and his immediate desire to return to his platoon. I was also extremely thankful for the medical equipment we had received upon deployment; the Israeli Bandage, the combat application (CAT) tourniquet, and Quickclot solution. These items, combined with our superb medical personnel from our HSS Company, a never-failing US Army helo MEDEVAC capability and our world-class Role 3 Hospital, saved many life and limb.

By morning of 29 March, I had spoken with brigade and expressed my desire to leave C/S 31 at FOB Wolf until the situation improved, and we began planning for a LAV reinforcement of the FOB. Specifics of the events of the previous night began to trickle in. After their insertion, the US and Canadian commanders had only a short time to coordinate roles and responsibilities before it became clear that large numbers (possibly over 100 hundred) Taliban were encircling the FOB. C/S 31 began to reinforce parts of the perimeter and prepared a reserve to move to endangered areas within the perimeter. The enemy then initiated a fierce volume of fire using mortars, RPGs, PKMs and AKs from dozens of individual fire positions from the North and Northwest of the FOB. C/S 31 moved the reserve group to reinforce a perimeter position in the Northern part of the FOB. In the darkness and dust, amidst the noise and confusion, this group of Canadians came under intense small arms fire, wounding three and killing Pte Robert Costall. The group commander was able to organize medical assistance, led by Maj Barry Ellis, M.D., and Capts Smith and Atwell took positive control and successfully extracted the casualties to the inner perimeter and to the helipad. Meanwhile the remainder of the garrison continued to engage the enemy. The decisive point of the defensive fight came when the Canadian Joint Target and Aerospace Control (JTAC), WO Cyr, coordinated a JDAM strike upon a compound containing 30 Taliban – killing them all and causing the others to realize that they could not win this fight. They withdrew by first light.

The ensuing day saw an improvement of the FOB defences and planning for our LAV reinforcement. However, an ominous event occurred which bothers me still. It became apparent that our casualties were possibly a result of friendly force fire from a US/ANA position. While I was aware of the possibility, I was never informed that a formal investigation into the incident commenced that day. A helicopter was despatched to FOB Wolf from Kandahar containing a US Army Colonel and a chaplain (who went to the FOB to administer pastoral support to US troops and to commemorate the loss of one of their soldiers). I was not informed of this helicopter trip and not invited to visit the beleaguered soldiers of C/S 31. Instead, a Canadian military police NCO was sent to begin the investigation. Our soldiers watched as the US Colonel and Chaplain provided leadership and moral support to their troops while the Canadian representative informed these tired and hurting troops that their casualties were possibly from a blue-on-blue and that they had to cooperate with him. They were furious at this insensitivity and lack of leadership. The investigative culture of Canadian Forces and garrison leadership pervaded this sad episode and overshadowed the tremendous courage and good combat skill displayed by our soldiers in the QRF role. While this meant nothing to others outside of TF Orion, it was extremely important to us, and began a separation between those of us involved in the fighting and bleeding, and those to whom these things remained abstract and inconsequential in adhering to garrison processes.

TF Orion sustained cohesion in hardship because trust had been established well before the fighting started, with a unit culture that promoted self-criticism and self-adjustment. I deliberately steered away from the tendency to order investigations into everything. This tendency was common-place in garrison in Canada; and while it gave the impression of transparency, it also strained investigative capabilities and became an easy-way out for commanders who sought to distance themselves from any possible problems within their units. I came to see this tendency as a distinctly careerist tool, that placed a CO well away from anything nasty, but which also diluted the moral authority of a CO and allowed him to escape the hard practice of moral problem-solving. An automatic default to outside investigations was also a statement of distrust in commanders who for the first time in half a century were dealing with the unknowns of combat. My response to the initial suggestion to investigate every single casualty from firefights was simple: when a man is wounded or killed on a battlefield, there is always a lot of blame to go around. War is messy, confusing, and unpredictable. Predictability and certainty are never achieved. Determining cause and effect is extremely difficult if not entirely impossible. To attempt to achieve certainty as a bureaucratic standard for every death would seriously erode trusts.

I am not suggesting in these statements that we tolerated breaches in the Code of Service Discipline or the Law of Armed Conflict. If I sensed that these were at issue, there was only one recourse – swift and decisive action. I was once advised by a legal officer that I was being too strict in sentencing soldiers in front of me in summary trial. Yet, I felt that discipline is the most important combat skill and clear boundaries had to be drawn, expectations had to be well announced and disseminated, and transgressions had to be firmly dealt with. This extended down to the seemingly trivialities of dress. I allowed soldiers to wear whatever load-carrying apparel, boots, and gloves they wished. But I also demanded that they wear CADPAT*, proper PPE* and IFF*; and took swift action when they did not. I would not tolerate the proliferation of platoon or

---

* CADPAT is the acronym for Canadian Disruptive Pattern, the camoflauge pattern unique to the CF.
* PPE: Personal Protective Equipment.
* IFF: Identification, Friend or Foe.

company badges or flags, as they jeopardize proper PPE and IFF, and because they reinforce sub-unit cohesion at the expense of Task Force cohesion.

It was beyond unit boundaries that things became more problematic, particularly after we became rather bloodied. Garrison investigative culture was antipathetic to our work in combat operations. We received orders to pass to the Military Police responsibility for ALL investigations for accidental and negligent discharges (ND). This delayed the expediency of summary trial and left soldiers languishing unnecessarily. It also served to diminish the authority of the chain of command. At other times, CF-sponsored investigations were conducted into unit affairs that I was not made aware of; which was synonymous to a vote of non-confidence. Such things breached the principles of mission command and of a trusting command climate. To help reduce the negative impacts and to reinforce the role and trust of commanders, I directed that with any discharge of weapons outside of firefights – from either negligent discharges or escalation of force – the company commander must inform me in writing within 24 hours the who, what, where, and when of the incident and to state whether or not they believed the incident required investigation for possible breach of the Rules of Engagement (ROE). I gave consideration to these statements and would act appropriately. As this order required automatic reaction and direct involvement of company commanders it served to reinforce their role, and to make us accountable for knowledge of subordinate actions, and compelled to promote battlefield discipline. The numbers of NDs and ROE escalations steadily diminished. In this manner it to a small degree helped reduce the garrison investigative mentality.

The incident at FOB Robinson (FOB Wolf was renamed FOB Robinson in April – in honour of the US SF soldier killed in Sangin in mid-March) also highlighted other important lessons for us. We needed more collective training in night battle, and the brigade needed common IFF standards for all units. The shortcuts taken in our training in Canada were beginning to catch up to us in theatre. Throughout our pre-deployment training we were denied access to sufficient number and types of night-fighting equipment, and we had no opportunity for night live-fire training. While we had attempted in January to correct this deficiency, we could only really master individual skills with the newly issued night equipment, and we could not effect a common standard of collective skill in the complex issue of night-time platoon, company, and battalion battle. After the FOB Robinson incident we looked hard at this, but the dispersion of our forces and the tempo of our operations precluded us from taking a pause and conducting such large-scale training. It fell to the sections and platoons to address this training delta whilst on operations.

On 31 March 2006, TF Orion began an impressive day and night manoeuvre to reinforce the small pressed garrison at FOB Robinson. Maj Fletcher's C Company was tasked to move to the FOB and remain there until the operational initiative was wrestled from the Taliban. When the executive order for this operation came (late afternoon), TF Orion was scattered across northern Kandahar province – 100 kilometres from KAF. We redeployed to KAF throughout that night, did a complete replenishment and proceeded on to the 150 kilometre move to FOB Robinson that morning, arriving by first light the next day after a nightmare of cross-country movement through terrain that was dense with previously destroyed vehicles from IEDs and ambushes. C Company arrived after first light, and I brought forward the TUAV detachment, artillery troop and re-supply column later that same morning. The reception was more than warm. The US SF soldiers and their US ETT and ANA soldiers were tired and feeling totally compromised. They had long since March 28th given up the idea of

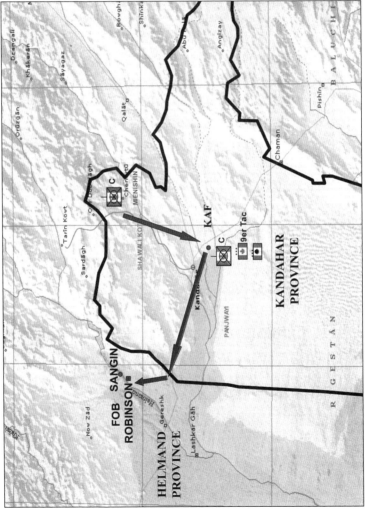

MAP 6: Op KETARA

regaining the tactical initiative. C Company was the proverbial US Cavalry arriving at the besieged wagon train. 40 armoured fighting vehicles accompanied by large cannons and professional infantry-man made everything change. This arrival commenced a five-week operation that saw C Company take complete control of Sangin District, dominating a hard-core Taliban area and pacifying the volatile region during a time of great vulnerability for UK forces just in the process of arriving into Helmand province. In retrospect, I began to appreciate how incredibly agile and capable was our LAV-based, M777-supported TF, able to manoeuvre long distances from our support base, sustain in harsh and austere conditions, and fight with overwhelming combat superiority. Several officers on the brigade staff observed this with critical and approving eye, and our lesson from this display of "operational reach" became valuable to subsequent events in July.

The brigade staff was adamant that C Company deploy to FOB Robinson under brigade control and I was warned not to accompany them. However, I did not trust in this. Although manned by very competent and determined officers, there was no one on the brigade headquarters who had any experience in a LAV infantry battalion or understood its logistical requirements or fighting capabilities. More seriously, there were no clear orders regarding C2 relationships between C Company and the US forces in FOB Robinson or UK forces in Helmand. I was very conscious of the potential for foreign officers to abuse the capability of a Canadian company. I was also conscious that the only people who would care about every detail of their support were my TF staff, and the staff of the National Support Element (NSE). This, coupled with the fact that I was determined that no Canadian soldier would ever be out of range of Canadian artillery in a fight, made me deploy forward with my tactical command convoy and a troop from A Battery. This allowed me to personally impose will and presence upon any element in FOB Robinson who might attempt to pull rank upon Maj Fletcher. It left me as the communications node between the brigade and the tactical fight, alleviating a burden from C Company. This also allowed my TAC CP to assume responsibility for coordinating the intelligence and enabler support to C Company. During subsequent operations in Helmand, we received a significant number of enablers and the position of 9er Tac between the fighting rifle company and the brigade proved effective. Maj Fletcher was able to exercise excellent sub-unit combat command without being overwhelmed by C2 and combat support coordination functions. Our use of 9er Tac as the intermediary HQ became a Standard Operating Procedure (SOP) for our subsequent operations. No matter how we transform in the future, we cannot afford to flatten the hierarchy to a point of overwhelming combat commanders who need to be on the ground with their soldiers, not tied to CPs.

C Company began an aggressive series of cordon and search and key leader operations for the next three weeks. Their first was to isolate and search the compound of a senior Taliban commander in Sangin District. This was the same compound approached by the US SF in late March, enroute to which they were decisively engaged and turned back with significant loss. In C Company's attempt to capture this leader, they were hindered by intelligence that kept giving different locations where he was hiding. As the company pulled out of FOB Robinson to move to their objective, word came through that his location had changed again. In an amazing feat of agility the entire company group switched focus while on the move at night, without lights and with minimal communications, and headed to a different objective area. Maj Fletcher quickly gave new orders, keeping the manoeuvre and coordinating measures simple and similar to his original concept of operations, allowing his Foreward Observation Officer (FOO), the imperturbable Capt Nichola Goddard to issue new control measure and fire support information after a brief map reconnaissance done in her LAV turret in the dark. The operation came off flawlessly. C Company narrowly missed capturing the Taliban leader, and shocked the Taliban C2 structure in Sangin. The only tense moments occurred after first light when word was spreading amongst villagers that Coalition Forces had infiltrated, and we witnessed hundreds of women and children exodus the objective area. We knew that Taliban fighters were present (we had good real-time intelligence of such), but this exodus became a better combat indicator of imminent trouble. However, the enemy did not mass and held their fire, preferring to keep weapons cached and instead stand and observe us unarmed and undistinguishable from the curious farmers who also gawked at us throughout.

In FOB Robinson, I remained with the Tac CP (at that point consisting of only 9er Tac LAV, G19er LAV, and E19er LAV with two support LUVWs) and helped to coordinate the enablers (several types of Electronic Warfare (EW) platforms, our artillery, our TUAV, AH, and CAS). I was being continuously fed intelligence updates by the US Army special operations commander whose CP I was parked beside. At this time I began to appreciate how modern technologies are coordinated and used at the BG level to support close operations. I affirmed my belief that the commander should be the nexus for all critical battlefield intelligence even while he is forward deployed on the battlefield. This function – intelligence collation in support of decision-making should not be abrogated to a staff officer or to another HQ (an ISTAR HQ for instance). I still firmly believe that the CO should be pushed real-time intelligence and be provided with the receivers – such as the UAV ground picture feed and translators to decode raw conversation intercepts. In a close fight, the commander is the best person to synthesize this material and use it to make decisions regarding movement and fires of his sub-units. To do this effectively, I thereafter increased the size of 9er Tac by adding a Bison CP with penthouse tent, signallers and at least one duty officer, a support Nyala (the RSM's vehicle) and – eventually – the Mobile Electronic Warfare Team (MEWT) vehicle.

During C Company's first cordon and search I received a 10 figure grid for a cellphone emission believed to be a Taliban commander. A US Apache pilot flying in support of C Company made visual contact with two persons sitting at that grid and radioed me to ask permission to engage. I denied his request. This incident demonstrated to me how complex combined arms operations could be prosecuted and the role of the BG commander in them. It also illustrated a case where the moral aspect of all decision-making is constant and critical. Despite an almost overwhelming desire to allow the Apache to engage a suspected target, I understood that this was loose interpretation of ROE and that my decision would be broadcast over the entire radio net, setting a very dangerous precedent for my subordinates. The moral correctness of battlefield decisions must standout on their own merit, and not have to be explained. This is sometimes very frustrating, but is the hallmark of counter-insurgency. On a separate occasion I was able to track on a UAV the movement of an insurgent group from the point where they initiated an ambush to a place where they stopped after they withdrew from the ambush (4 kilometres away), and directed that they be engaged and killed with missile fire. This incident demonstrated the advantage of having robust ROE and the requirement for having the CO empowered to make hard decisions based on his personal contact with intelligence (UAV feed in this case) that gives him certainty about the moral correctness of his decision.

C Company repeated demonstrations of strength and will frequently in the next four weeks, maintaining complete initiative and disrupting all Taliban attempts to mass and attack. They had several bloody skirmishes that resulted in enemy dead and wounded. One of these involved C/S 31, fresh from QRF duties and back in their LAVs and assigned again to C Company. A month after they had taken casualties at FOB Robinson they exacted revenge when in escorting a night supply convoy to the FOB in late April they detected through thermal sights an enemy group setting up an ambush along the route just over a kilometre from their advance guard. The LAVs took up fire positions silently, coordinated fire control orders and initiated lethal bursts upon the unsuspecting enemy. One enemy pickup truck and 14 fighters were destroyed. Happier, C/S 31 realized in the post fight the sad truth that no amount of enemy dead could make up for our few but precious losses.

During Operation Ketara we learned for the first time the benefit of OEF enablers (helos, strike aircraft, and various EW and imagery platforms). Up until that point we had not been briefed upon or trained with US air-based intelligence, reconnaissance or surveillance assets, and were fairly ignorant of electronic warfare capabilities. It fell to a US Army SF Captain to give me speed lessons on each type of capability, its characteristics, and how best to employ it. I was grateful for this knowledge and desirous to share the lesson learned with Canadian trainers.

On Operation Ketara we also came to understand the limitations of the myriad of enablers that might come our way. The brigade did not have sufficient numbers of enablers to cover every task, and our operations were normally of lower priority than any of the time-sensitive HVT hunts being conducted by special forces. Therefore, even when we were allocated several enablers, they were often stripped away very early in an operation, leaving us relatively deaf and blind and with sinking feelings as they departed each time. When they were present, they provided useful intelligence and support, and made us feel more secure. But they were also plagued with the friction normal in combat: incompatibility of technologies; air gaps; low fidelity sensors; receivers that were not rugged enough for combat; vehicle and equipment breakdown; bad atmospherics and foul weather; restrictions on intelligence sharing that are inherent in coalition operations; and human error. Friction degraded our sensor and communications networks to the point where they were incapable of producing more than a fleeting glimpse of a portion of the enemy's force; temporary visibility upon only one piece of an immense and dynamic jigsaw puzzle. While desirous for enablers, I began to place more reliance on bottom-up intelligence from Afghan sources, and in our own integral support capabilities.

Concept of Operations – Fixing the Enemy: Panjwayi and Mountain Thrust

May came, and with it the slow realization that the *Dushman* were massing in central Kandahar. We initially believed that this concentration was entirely about harvesting and moving poppy and hash crops. I informed my superiors of this belief, and regretted doing so the following month when it was clear that the Taliban were staying. It was not until late May that we began to believe Afghan opinion that the enemy's intent was to attack Kandahar City in what would be a catastrophic statement of strength. However, my first report from April seemed to work against me, and I found that there was no appetite amongst higher staffs for negative reporting (particularly at the division level) because my message countered their estimate of the enemy situation and jeopardized the detailed planning they were pursuing for Operation Mountain Thrust, which would take us away form Zharie/Panjwayi again and again during June and July. We became very concerned about losing Kandahar during these months. By then we were into significant combat operations in Zharie and Panjwayi, but operating – for the most part – without enablers and support.

After the episode of 14 April (involving the death of ANP), our B Company had operated extensively in the districts. On 28 April, while I was on leave, my Deputy Commanding Officer (Maj Tod Strickland) commanded an operation into southern Zharie – ostensibly probing for the enemy. As his command post vehicles were moving into a position in the Arghandab River wadi, the lead vehicle became stuck in soft sand. All vehicles from the packet then came under intense and accurate small arms fire from positions on the north bank of the river. Without hesitation, and at significant personal risk, RSM Northrup, and MCpl Jason Froude, leapt over the back deck of the LAV III and began to organize and execute recovery operations while the remaining vehicles began to engage the enemy. The fire was of such intensity that an ANP vehicle, immediately to the rear of where the pair were working, was immobilized when a RPG struck the back of the pick-up truck. For approximately twenty minutes, the whole time under fire, CWO Northrup orchestrated the recovery of 9er Tac, ground-guiding vehicles and controlling the movement of personnel, while also identifying targets and sources of fire and liaising with the ANP in an effort to assist them in the recovery of their damaged vehicle. This action confirmed to us that this enemy, unlike all those we had met thus far, would stand and fight in broad daylight. It also demonstrated to all ranks, the competency and courage of their RSM.

Upon my return from leave in May we began deliberate planning for a series of operations that would take place in Zharie-Panjwayi between mid-May and mid-June. I conducted a reconnaissance into the heart of Zharie on 14 May to find Capt Massoud living there with approximately 60 ANP "fighters" using the ancient fort of Ghundy Ghar to dominate western Zharie and to protect a school that had been threatened by the Taliban. He and his men were tired. They had been in contact with Taliban groups frequently and had some successes in killing a senior enemy commander – Mullah Baqi – and capturing other subordinate commanders. One of these was Mullah Abrahim (or Ibrihim in some translations), a tough old mujhadin who was notorious for his skill with mines and RPGs. Later on, I was able to cultivate a relationship with Abrahim while he convalesced in our hospital at KAF. I visited him frequently, brought him beloved chocolate and tea, and engaged in rather pleasant conversation. Through this contact I led him toward acceptance of the government's amnesty program, during which he reinforced our information operations campaign by publicly denouncing the Taliban at a well-attended press conference. I personally thought that this amnesty program was our best hope for success in the south, but it received insufficient financial resourcing to gain traction.

Massoud had also succeeded in establishing a network of informants in the region, using gifted cellphones and reward money for information about Taliban movements. I witnessed the effectiveness of this network and from 17 May onward, I incorporated Capt Massoud into my tactical command post as a liaison officer and this provided me with direct access to his HUMINT network. The only difficulties we encountered with this intelligence stemmed from cultural differences; our reliance upon maps and grid references was strange to the Afghan, who gave location and direction relative to the compounds of prominent locals and village names – many of which were not on our maps. They would describe locations in terms of "the gardens" or "the traffic circle" in remote towns and could not determine north, south, east or west, only the terms above and below. I taught Capt Massoud to read a map and use grid references, and provided topographical maps to him and his subordinates so that we could coordinate better. However, the informants could not have or use these maps, necessitating therefore a transliteration by us of their information to a map reference. This continued to be a problem throughout our fighting between May and August. It is unfortunate that we could not have issued the informants simple commercial GPS phones to allow them to read grids to us.

During my reconnaissance on 14 May, I promised Massoud relief within a few days. We began movements on 16 May after dark fell, and by 17 May both B and C Companies were in Zharie/Panjwayi. Thus began Operation Bravo Guardian, with the intent of clearing a triangular area around the townships of Nalgham. C Company (minus one platoon) and ANP forces were put into blocking positions to the West and North. My tactical command post and a troop from A Battery were in a blocking position on the Northwest of the objective, co-located with the ANP command element on the Ghundy Ghar fort feature – with excellent observation of the area. Massoud told me when we began manoeuvring that morning that we would be fighting within 30 minutes – guaranteed. He was off by only 4 minutes.

Capt Jay Adair commanded B Company in the absence of the regular Officer Commanding, Maj Nick Grimshaw, who had just departed for leave. Earlier on the morning of 17 May, despite orders that had prepared Capt Adair and his company to operate in Nalgham, I redeployed them, without advanced warning and without time for battle procedure, to clear out enemy seen in Pashmul, in Zharie District. They entered that complex of villages at approximately 10 AM, and soon one of the attached platoons (C/S 32 – 8 Platoon from C Company) became involved in a fierce firefight with a large Taliban force. This fight lasted another 2 hours, during which B Company synchronized artillery and AH support, and led the clearance operation of the objective. With the attached ANA soldiers, the company then commenced subsequent detailed clearance operations resulting in the capture of 32 suspected Taliban fighters and found evidence of Taliban mass casualty evacuation. Just prior to last light the battle turned against B Company when Taliban forces ambushed 5 Platoon, killing an ANA soldier and the Company's Forward Observer Controller. At that time six platoons of the BG (both B and C Companies) were involved in separate firefights, stressing our command and control. Capt Adair took firm control of his company and, even though he was again personally under fire, he organized the successful extraction of 5 Platoon, consolidated the company, and remained on the battlefield to conduct attacks by fire against Taliban compounds, using direct and indirect fire, AH, and fixed wing support. Recommencing offensive manoeuvres as soon as possible the following morning, B Company found that the enemy had withdrawn. These were the first BG-level combat days of the tour and were marked by numerous engagements, the first use of artillery and air in support of fierce close-quarter combat, and by casualties and prisoners. They were trials of professionalism and determination, during which the performance of all participating – but especially acting company commanders Jay Adair and Ryan Jurkowski – was exemplary. It was telling that the first Battalion-level combat in 50 years was conducted – almost entirely – by junior officers, WOs, NCOs, and soldiers.

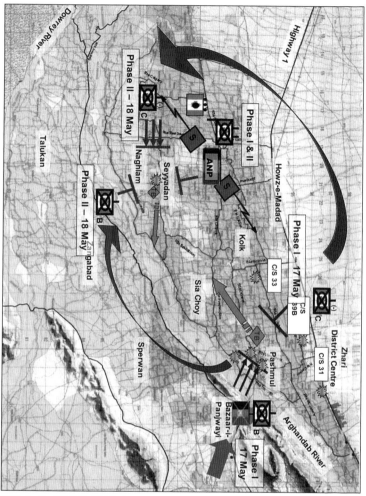

MAP 7: Op BRAVO GUARDIAN, 17-18 May

This first battle of Pashmul cost us dearly. Capt Goddard was killed in action by enemy fire in the ambush upon 5 Platoon. At the time she had been engaging in battle since early morning, coordinating direct fire, indirect fire, and AH support for soldiers of B and C Companies fighting Taliban groups entrenched in the village complex of Pashmul. Her actions at the time of death were characteristic of all of her activities throughout the period January to May 2006. She had served as the FOO with C and B Companies and in the performance of her duties Capt Goddard lived almost continuously in the field, in austere FOBs, and in company leaguers situated routinely in open fields near remote villages; always in the vicinity of known enemy sanctuaries. In such circumstances, sleeping on the ground under the stars and working in conditions of extreme heat and dust, she led her FOO party with a superb mix of cheerfulness and competence. As a matter of course her FOO party would move independent of the company to observe and register artillery and air support targets, almost daily exposing them to Taliban attack. During operation Sola Kowel she performed dismounted FOO functions at high altitude in support of the battalion clearance of the Sahmahardan Ghar (the "Belly Button") Mountains. During five weeks of operations in Sangin District in Helmand Province, Capt Goddard volunteered on at least four occasions to conduct reconnaissance operations into villages where only weeks before the Taliban had effected devastating attacks upon coalition forces. Working with only limited TF support, and remaining long hours in positions exposed to enemy observation and fire, she defined the objective areas, confirmed company group approaches and, for the first time since the Korean War, executed high explosive and illumination fire missions in support of Canadian troop manoeuvres against a known enemy. In addition, she coordinated a complex mix of artillery, aircraft, and electronic warfare assets, with technical perfection and with unwavering calmness that won for her complete trust and respect of all ranks. Her willingness to volunteer for dangerous tasks, her acceptance of risk in continual presence of the enemy, and her continuous demonstration of the highest leadership skills parallel the highest manifestations of leadership and courage in Canadian military history.

It is unfortunate that in the aftermath of losing Capt Goddard, when we were considering her for an award, we had to factor in that the award might be construed by many as attributable to her being a woman. That we even had such thoughts is testimony to how far we still have to go before gender integration is truly achieved. For the Afghans, they accepted her status as a warrior much more easily. In subsequent discussions with Pashtu elders, Capt Goddard was compared to a famous Afghan woman who fought with distinguished bravery against the British at Maywand (a 19th century battlefield only 30 kilometres from Pashmul). On another occasion an elder told me that it was indicative of Canada's love for Afghanistan that we would ask our women to fight here for the Afghan people (in Pashtu society women are to be always protected from danger).

We were forced to withdraw from operations in Zharie-Panjwayi when it became a temporary joint special operations area (JSOA) between 18-23 May. We returned on 24 May to conduct BDA (battle-damage assessment) patrols and to clear areas where Massoud's informants told us the enemy were occupying or transiting through. This included Pashmul, Siah Choy, Kolk, Nalgham, Mushan, Talukan, and Zangibad. Of these, Pashmul was the most troublesome as it allowed easy access to both Panjwayi District Centre and to Highway 1, where ambush attacks were becoming more frequent and deadly.

We recommenced our work in Zharie with Operation Yadgar, with B and C Companies again executing TF offensive operations in Pashmul. This time C Company was the manoeuvre force while B Company set blocking positions west of Pashmul. At approximately 1600 hours on 24 May, after supporting C Company's detailed clearance of four Pashmul villages, Six Platoon (B Company) came under fire from an enemy during a meeting engagement, wherein one of our G-Wagons was struck by multiple RPGs, seriously wounding the platoon interpreter – "Junior" – (removing both his legs). Only through the quick actions of MCpl Fitzgerald and the platoon leadership did 6 Platoon manage to extract with few casualties. Capt Adair organized the MEDEVAC of the wounded, and the establishment of an effective defensive position on the battlefield that night, incorporating C Company – commanded by Capt Ryan Jurkowski, (Maj Fletcher still being on leave).

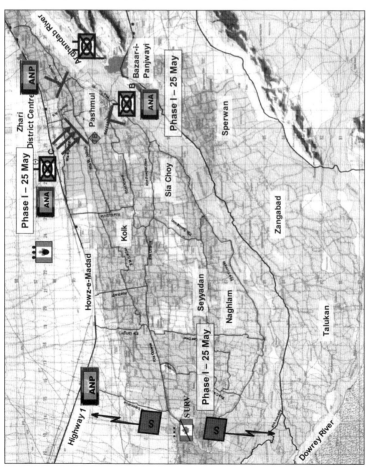

MAP 8a: Op YADGAR, 25 May

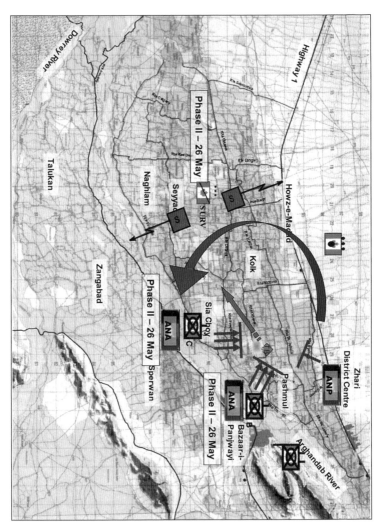

MAP 8b: Op YADGAR, 26 May

At the time, I sat in an overwatch position above the Arghandab River on a prominent ridge line, a site that looked out over all of Pashmul and which provided good communications. From here we could apply fire from our LAVs onto the east of Pashmul,

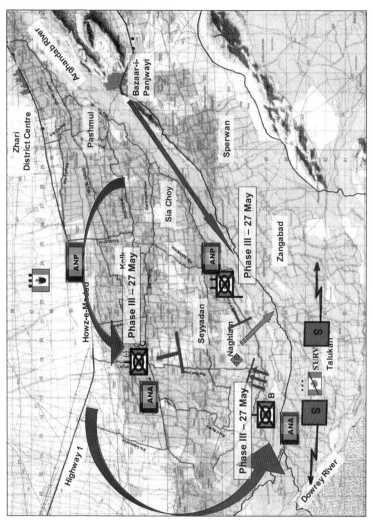

MAP 8c: Op YADGAR, 27 May

protect the LOC for the companies across the Arghandab, and exert positive control over the application of artillery fire and air support. With me was Capt Massoud, connected to his cellphone informant network. He gave me information during the evening's

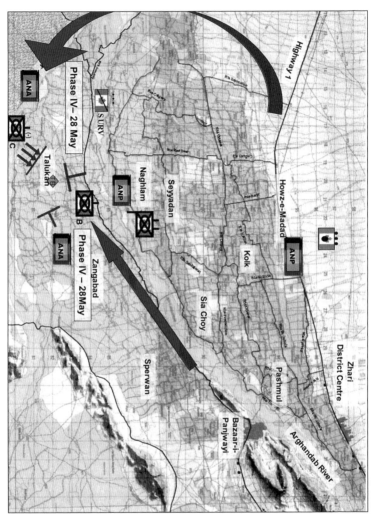

MAP 8d: Op YADGAR, 28 May

fighting that suggested the enemy was held up in the Shakor Ghun-
di feature west of Pashmul, and in Siah Choy, to the southwest.
That night I issued orders redirecting the manoeuvre, pushing
B Company from Pashmul west and C Company from Siah Choy

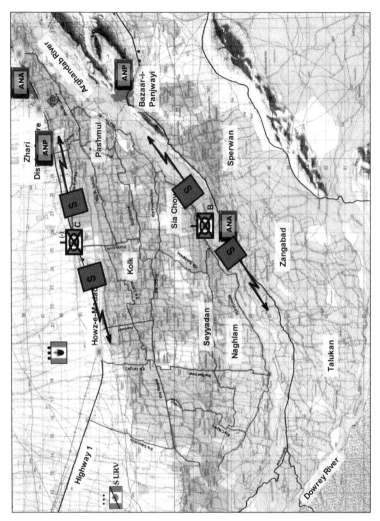

MAP 8e: Op YADGAR, 29 May-7 June

northeast, with surveillance troop and ANP in blocking positions. On 25 May B Company advanced west toward Shakor Ghundi in an attempt to trap the Taliban forces encountered the previous day. They achieved this effect by responding quickly to an engagement of their lead element and – operating dismounted – manoeuvred two platoons to position where they pinned the enemy in place with direct and indirect fire. Meanwhile Capt Jurkowski led C Company through the village of Siah Choy to begin detailed clearance operations. At approximately 1030 hrs I ordered him to move his soldiers to conduct an assault onto a series of grape drying huts and compounds where B Company had the Taliban force pinned down. Despite temperatures above 40 degrees Celsius, C Company conducted a long dismounted advance to the assault position and attacked the enemy from the south, clearing north in the wake of deadly accurate fire provided by our M777, and by B Company supporting platoons. The result was one enemy confirmed killed, the capturing of 11 suspected Taliban fighters, and evidence indicating another dozen Taliban casualties which were reported to us on enemy ICOM chatter. The following day, I was shown 9 fresh graves south of Shakur Gundy. The enemy also had multiple casualties and we attempted to intercept the cars that carried them from Zharie westward to Helmand, to no avail.

On 25 May, B and C Companies again set night defensive positions on the battlefield, an important psychological practice. It demonstrated to the enemy that we would not leave – that we were prepared to stay and sustain our pressure upon them. With our nightly re-supply, we demonstrated an apparently inexhaustible supply of manpower, vehicles, ammunition, water, and fuel. This was a deliberate posture adopted by the NSE Commander, LCol John Conrad, who desired to play upon the psyche of the enemy by portraying fathomless depth in our sustainment capability, using frequent robust combat re-supply columns to us, stockpiling massive stores in positions where the enemy could observe them, extracting every damaged vehicle from the fight within hours and replacing it, or fixing it on the battlefield in short time, showing to the *Dushman* that all of his significant efforts to hurt us were having so little impact. The cumulative effect was that the enemy, whose logistics and medical chain was so thin, could only engage us in combat for up to 36 hours before they were forced to withdraw. By the morning of 26 May the remaining enemy in the Pashmul area again moved away. With thin intelligence leads from Massoud's network, we chased these elusive groups for 4 more days, conducting offensive manoeuvres all across Zharie and Panjwayi districts, resulting with only minor fleeting skirmishes.

After these manoeuvres and fights, on the afternoon of 28 May, I conducted a comprehensive After-Action Report (AAR) in the field with all key leaders in a pastoral orchard along the banks of the Arghandab River. We had learned much.

We learned that once we had found the enemy, we needed to fix him with fires and finish him in close-quarter combat. Neither of these things was easy. It required us to stay within 100-150 metres of him and to coordinate fires before physically moving to clear his positions. Doing so was contrary to human nature. The degree of success we had in close quarter combat became personality-dependent. The majority of soldiers when fired upon for the first time would seek to disengage back toward the "last safe place" they had occupied. After several encounters they repressed this urge but would be very reluctant to advance in contact (especially when separated from their LAVs). Forward movement, or staying in place, on the close-quarter battlefield (especially after night-fall) depended upon the continued presence of battalion and company commanders, supported by the "natural fighters" in our ranks. It had become evident to me that the number of true fighters we had was a small minority. By fighter,

I mean those men and women predisposed to keep fighting regardless of violence and danger; those who repressed fear not just because they wanted to remain with their primary group, but because of an overwhelming desire to beat the enemy; those who truly wanted to hunt the enemy and make him the victim. I would estimate that there were only 6 or 7 such individuals in every forty-man platoon. Yet, their stalwartness almost always became the psychological pivot point for the action of a section, platoon or company engaged in intensive battle. I came to rely upon the determination of commanders and this small number of fighters in each platoon and company to override the natural fear of close-quarter battle and to ensure that we kept the enemy fixed before closing to finish him. Trust was the essential element. The moral authority of the commanders, not their rank or appointment, was essential in this fighting, and the moral judgement of commanders and their personal example was required every minute to keep our troops moving forward in places fraught with danger. There was no place for careerist considerations on this battlefield.

After the first battlefield AAR, I returned to KAF to inform the brigade of our estimates of enemy strength and designs in Zharie/Panjwayi. The brigade staff was interested and I was invited on the evening of 29 May to sit with General Freakley and inform him of our operations. He was also very interested, but a little disconcerted that his staff had not identified such a massing of enemy. He appreciated that this enemy was not targeted in the planning for Operation Mountain Thrust, the very large-scale Division operation about to commence. He realized that Mountain Thrust would order my forces away from Zharie/Panjwayi to move back into the mountains of Showali-kot and Khakrez. He listened to my suggestion that we change our focus and stay in Zharie/Panjwayi. He countered that we should leave the bulk of our attached ANA in those districts and proceed with small numbers of ANA to the north. When I informed him that we only had a maximum of 15-20 ANA he became very angry, largely about not being aware of this shortfall. This surprised me deeply, because we had made it a daily point to complain about a lack of ANA resources. The net result of this meeting was a disgruntled commander, a divisional staff that began to spin doctor the information we gave them regarding Zharie/Panjwayi, and a weak directive to "do all you can do" in those districts before we were required to go north. I directed B and C Companies to remain in the field until 8 June, conducting platoon manoeuvres, and be ready for another Task Force push on 10 June. During this period the companies remained very active, encountering Taliban ambush groups (whom they were hunting) every other night, and incrementally reducing their numbers.

Operation Jagra

Operation Jagra commenced on 10 June with a broad and sweeping deception manoeuvre of C Company out to Helmand, then a night time movement south and back eastward following the Dowrey River to enter the Zharie/Panjwayi area by first light from the west on the 12th of June. This completely surprised the enemy. B Company was in blocking positions, along with Surveillance troop, 9er Tac, and the ANP. Upon moving into Nalgham on 12th June, C Company trapped a group of Taliban in the village of Seyyedan, and proceeded over the course of three hours to incrementally inflict casualties until the remnants to that group escaped with their dead and wounded. Typically, after 24-36 hours of fighting the enemy gave up resistance and melted away. This action cost us two severely wounded (Cpl Ozerkevic and Pte Ginther), hit by small arms fire in close-quarter assault upon an enemy position. We subsequently destroyed part of this Taliban force, but it was extremely difficult to chase them. Our intelligence sources consisted of periodic radio-fed information bites from our All Source Intelligence Centre in KAF, and more frequent cellphone messages by informants to Capt Massoud. While he attempted to keep us abreast of where

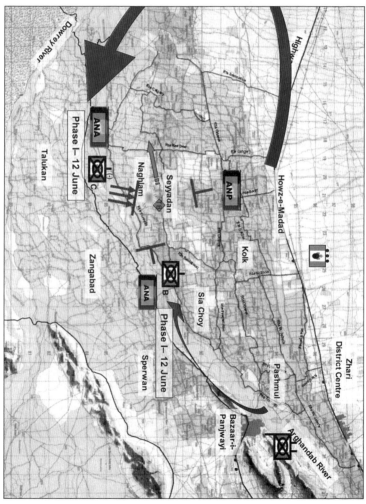

MAP 9a: Op JAGRA, June 11-12

the battered group was moving, the lack of grid or map references made tracking the group shear guesswork. They could move quickly on foot, with impunity, along the covered irrigation ditches, while we had to be cautious with every movement, constantly treating each

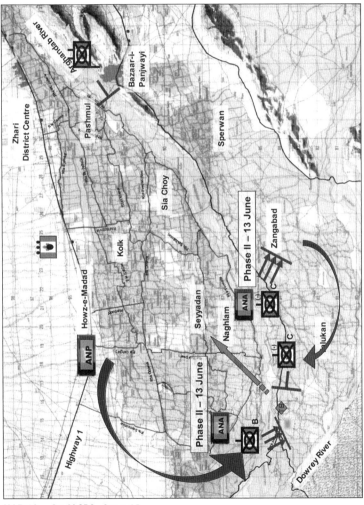

MAP 9b: Op JAGRA, June 13

corner as a possible ambush position or IED site. Without any type of aerial support, maintaining contact with this fleeing enemy was impossible in the close country of Zharie-Panjwayi.

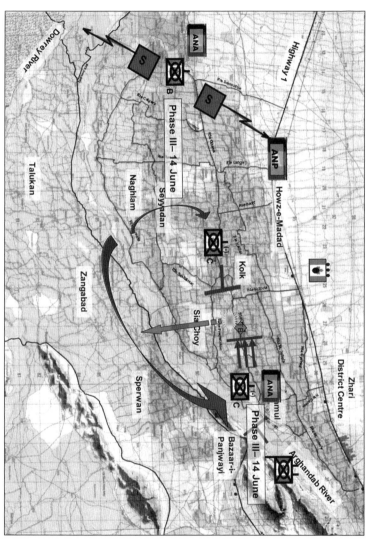

MAP 9c: Op JAGRA, June 13

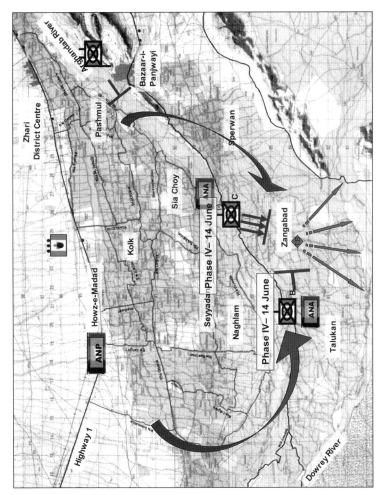

MAP 9d: Op JAGRA, June 14

But we continued manoeuvres to re-establish contact with him anyway, and to disrupt his plans and deny him freedom of movement, using B and C companies alternatively as blocking and strike forces. On June 14th we were ordered out of the districts, to move north to begin Operation Mountain Thrust. B Company stayed behind to maintain a presence in Zharie-Panjwayi, while C Company,

9er Tac, and surveillance troop travelled northward in night deception moves to linkup on the objective – the town of Chinar – with A
Company and the supporting troop from A Battery. We then spent
4 days attempting to find the Taliban that the Division was so adamant was there. They had left before we arrived.

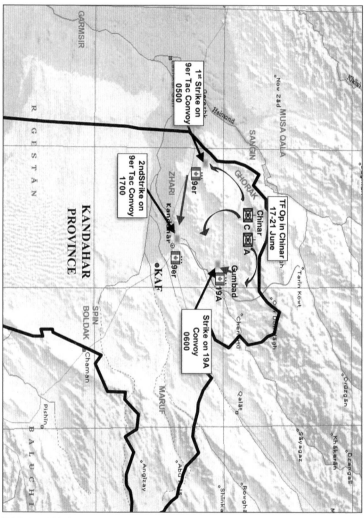

MAP 10: IED Strikes, 22 June

At the end of Operation Jagra I ordered all components of the A
and C Companies to disperse and manoeuvre across northern Kandahar and attempt to confuse the enemy as much as possible. In this
effort we lost several good men from the fight when C/S 39A was
struck by an IED near Shinkay, wounding the Company Second-in-
Command (2IC) of A Company, the superb Capt Martin Larosse,
and his incredible gunner Cpl Ryan Elrick. Martin suffered
severe trauma to his feet, Elrick lost the lower half of each leg.
I visited them in the hospital that night. Martin was dreary with
drugs – but positive and thankful to live. Elrick was lucid and hum-
bling. In the few short hours since the amputation of both legs,
he had taken stock and reformulated his life plans. He ran through
with me how he would adjust, what his new goals were, how he
would reach each one, and what opportunities he felt might
now avail themselves to him. I was reduced to adoration of this
mature, strong, and unbreakable spirit.

Other lives held in the balance that day. I had decided to take 9er
Tac in a deception manoeuvre west through Ghorak District while A
and C Companies manoeuvred eastward. This was remote and hos-
tile territory, seldom assailed by us, and I wanted to move through it
very quickly and reach Maywand by dark. However, five blown tires
forced our column to linger on a ridgeline in the extremely beautiful
Gamarbak valley, obvious to the enemy. We employed deception as
best we could, but it is no easy thing to hide an armoured vehicle
column. The next day, with tires repaired we proceeded south to
Maywand, only to strike an IED just after first light. I had no doubt
that the enemy were tracking us (something confirmed by our intelligence people later that day). The IED struck the vehicle behind
me, G19, engulfing us all in flame and smoke and causing a mobility
kill – but no serious injuries. After the blast we conducted an anti-
ambush drill, firing at the button man – whom we could see fleeing

southward on a motorbike. We pursued to a village where I dismounted and stormed in, accompanied by Capt Massoud and one other soldier. I was angry. Massoud was livid. He pursued the suspect only to lose trace in the confusion of compounds and orchards. I gathered several local elders, sat them down and proceeded with shura. While I initially felt threatening and desirous of compensations, I reverted quickly to a quiet and deliberate approach when I saw the resigned and victimized expressions of these old men. They could offer little except to say that without our permanent presence here, there was very little they could do to stop IED attacks. My shift in emotions was not unique, I queried many of our soldiers who had endured the same experiences; ambush or attack followed within an hour by local shura, where there was no place for the anger or desire for revenge that might characterize the attitude and reaction of soldiers from other nations. I marvelled at the ability of the Canadian soldier to suffer and not exact wrongful revenge. I was coming to understand the absolute essential quality of emotional control in battle. The term "shots fired in anger" are so apt. When fired upon, there is an initial seething anger created that if not checked quickly can invoke rage. I witnessed how some other nations reacted to IED or ambush by firing at everything around them in anger and fear, using fire as an emotional steam valve. Commanders must watch for, and train for, the curtailment of angered responses. It is not wrong to fire in contact, it is wrong to continue to do so long after the contact ends.

It took eight hours for us to recover G19. Early in the wait Capt Massoud brought to me a Taliban cleric who he had found passing by us on the back of a motorbike. His driver was a local farmer. The cleric was originally from a nearby village, but now lived in Pakistan, teaching young Talibs in a madrassa. He was not a fighter. He accepted my offer to stay with us during the recovery; on condition we would fix the intermittent engine of his driver's bike. I felt that his presence would dissuade further attack upon our exposed column, but what I really wanted was information. We talked for three hours, during which I heard his story of preaching and belief (without mention of any hatred of us), and made him listen to my stories of my children, with pictures, and slowly and as persuasively as possible, our version of the Afghan struggle, so that at some time in the future he could personalize his preaching. We parted on good enough terms, his motorbike accompanying us until we linked up with a platoon from B Company and some ANP.

When the recovery was effected we proceeded toward KAF; however, on the western outskirts of Kandahar City we were again attacked by a suicide vehicle-borne IED. The blast sent shrapnel and flame over us, and my alternate crew commander, MCpl Gregory White, standing in the back hatch, had the lower part of his left arm severely damaged. He reported his state to us on intercom. We stopped and applied three tourniquets to his damaged arm. I organized the convoy, assembled the wounded and directed yet another recovery of damaged vehicles. White's situation deteriorated and the medics informed me that with his blood loss, he might not last until helicopter MEDEVAC. I did not like this area as a dust-off location anyway, and I sensed possible subsequent attacks. I decided to risk the ground evacuation of MCpl White to the PRT compound where Canadian doctors could perform better initial treatment, and where there was a secure helipad.

My LAV parted company from the convoy and Stitch (Cpl Hayward) drove through the dark but crowded streets of Kandahar unescorted, at good speed, with amazing skill and sensitivity to both vehicle and pedestrians, while our gunner Cpl Greg Davis warned away local traffic with voice and air horn. We arrived at Camp

Nathan Smith in time to treat White to an IV drip before the US bird came in to evacuate him. I helped carry his stretcher to the bird and bid him a brotherly farewell, happy that he would live, and proud of the performance of his brother crewmembers. We then travelled back to KAF to visit the wounded and take stock.

It became clear in subsequent days that 9er Tac was being targeted, and that the ANP were passing information to the enemy regarding our movements. We had suspected this. I was not really bothered by this targeting. It had the positive effect of demonstrating that rank and appointment did not exonerate me from risk. However, I felt extremely bad for my crews, who would have to suffer the consequences of working in the 9er Tac convoy. We informed everyone that the risks were high and said we would understand if anyone wanted a transfer to another assignment for the remainder of the tour, without stigma – as each one of them had already endured full measure. No one asked to be re-assigned. I led the column out again the next day (I always crew commanded the lead vehicle) in order to keep everyone from dwelling on this. While we were very crafty in our movements and route choices before June 22nd, we were devious thereafter. I changed plans on a whim, deviated all practices, never conformed to any patterns of movement, and often travelled at night with constantly changing light configuration on the vehicles, sometimes having the second vehicle only with headlights on (providing oncoming drivers with a massive and frightening silhouette of my front LAV), sometimes with three vehicles with lights on, sometimes without any lights – depending on traffic and streetlight conditions. We changed headlight configuration at each corner and over each hillcrest, making it very difficult for enemy to track us. We were never hit again.

Operation Mountain Thrust again put us into Northern Kandahar for the last part of June, this time in Mienishin District, in the troublesome town of Chenartu. While we were operating in Mienishin, B Company remained busy in Zharie/Panjwayi. They patrolled aggressively and were successful in reintroducing several reconstruction efforts in the districts. However, the enemy was not about to give up their design on this terrain. On the night of 23 June they attempted to attack a B Company patrol base set up at last light in the Arghandab River wadi just north of the school in Mushan, Panjwayi. But LAV gunners, using night vision sights were able to alert our troops, so that with the initiation of some enemy fire, the response of the LAVs was decisive and devastating. Several enemy withdrew westward toward the protection of the school, where OC B Company, Maj Grimshaw, had already despatched a section of infantry who were able to finish the Taliban force. The negative effect of this was to force a cancellation of a village medical outreach program scheduled for the following day. The night of the 24th of June saw B Company again in operations, attempting to assist a US special operations force unit that had had a bad fight in Pashmul. When I returned from northern Kandahar Province we began deliberate planning for yet another large TF operation in the Pashmul area.

Conceding that there were indeed enemy in the Zharie/Panjwayi districts, the Division allowed us to go back there in early July to fight. They allowed us to deviate from the stated objective areas of Operation Mountain Thrust in order to further disrupt Taliban massing in the areas closest to Kandahar; but only for a few days. Despite the signs of Taliban concentrations in these key areas, the Division bent to other pressures. The British had become hard pressed in the Helmand River Valley, especially around Sangin, where they occupied FOB Robinson and a beleaguered platoon house at the Sangin District Centre. This second force was finding things very difficult, with daily attacks and a very weak helicopter re-supply system. Operation Mountain Thrust changed focus and planned for a brigade-sized operation (Operation Hewad) into the Sangin area to eliminate the threat there. As a preliminary phase, TF Orion, supported by an unprecedented number of ANA (150) and 100 ANP, and with the UK Household Cavalry troop attached, would spend 3-4 days in Pashmul to disrupt Taliban activity there before moving to Helmand to assist the British in Operation Hewad. Our preliminary phase was called Operation Zahar. It was carefully planned with the hope of finally being able to mass sufficient forces in a small area to allow for the complete encirclement of an enemy force, and their complete destruction. I wanted to approach an enemy group from three or four sides simultaneously and prevent their escape. This would mean employment of all three companies (with two platoons each). This would be the first time that a three rifle company operation would occur, the benefits of which became evident immediately.

There were reports of Taliban weapons and ammunition caches in cemeteries, of clinics in a local "doctor's compound", and of narcotics labs in Zhaire District. There were probably 5 groups of Taliban operating here. The decision as to which enemy group we should strike, and where, was made by OC B Company. For almost two months, he and his company had operated in this area and they had a sense of the enemy there akin to how a beat cop knows his streets. While there was no hard intelligence indicating such, Maj Grimshaw "felt" certain that we would find the enemy, or something valuable to him, around the large cemetery complex in Shakur Ghundy in Pashmul.

This was axiomatic. In exercising the *sense* function I relied less and less on an inventory of ISTAR* sensors and more and more upon personal *sense* of where the enemy was, what he intended to do, and how he could be deceived. TF leaders personally reconnoitred districts and analyzed local HUMINT sources to identify trends and to guess if an enemy was in a general area (almost always this was relayed to us as a 20-40 man Taliban group hiding in the vicinity of a particular village). We then attempted to manoeuvre into that district quietly under cover of darkness, using deception, and – as much as possible – isolate the village by using thin blocking and cut off forces. We would conduct manoeuvre (cordon and searches) and fires (show of force artillery or 25mm fire) to produce enemy ICOM chatter, and from this ICOM chatter (or HUMINT from local nationals), we would attempt to vector in upon the enemy's locations. However, in the end, finding him was almost always a result of advance-to-contact in the close country where he hid, and was confirmed by the exchange of fire at close quarters.

We began operation ZAHAR on the night of 7th July. As a deception we had A Company and Recce Platoon conduct a relief in place with B Company in Patrol Base Wilson along Highway One and we moved B Company under darkness to Panjwayi District centre. None of this movement constituted anything irregular from activities we had done in the preceding months. Then we carefully staged C Company through Kandahar city, and then blackout drive to Panjwayi District Centre. 9er Tac followed closely behind. As I brought the column up onto the high ridge overlooking Pashmul, all three companies and Recce Platoon were advancing toward the objective – Objective Puma. They advanced in the minutes just after midnight, long columns of vehicles moving slowly, without

---

* ISTAR: Intelligence, Surveillance, Target Acquisition and Reconnaissance.

light, and emitting little noise, a virtue of the LAV. We had embedded several ANA soldiers in each section, in our LAVs, and held the rest back in reserve. The ANA cannot move in their pickup trucks at night without using lights, so it is better to leave them out of initial break-in battles.

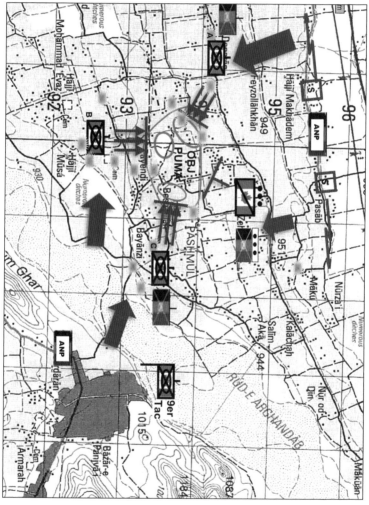

MAP 11: Op ZAHAR, July 7-10

The battle plan called for all three companies to move mounted and dismounted at night to encircle Objective Puma – Shakur Gundey. Before we left KAF we had received a visit from the NDS chief who gave us information about the position of four early warning groups that might interfere with our advance. His information proved to be extremely accurate. Within 20 minutes after we initiated our four pronged advance, Recce Platoon had three detainees and all three rifle companies were engaging enemy early warning groups with 25mm LAV fire. 9er Tac had just crested the ridge where I would establish my command post and we were setting up our radio remotes when the **BOOM-BOOM-BOOM** of LAV fire erupted to our front in three locations, signifying the joining of battle of each manoeuvre sub-unit. I began to receive contact reports and to discern the enemy with my night sites and binoculars. This began what was to be a twelve hours running engagement with Taliban forces that saw us move slowly but steadily inward to the objective.

The enemy was surprised by our night manoeuvre and advance, but had time and terrain to their advantage. They watched our advance and laid ambushes where they thought best, but were dissuaded by our steadily closing encirclement. Most of our many contacts were against groups caught in hiding, or attempting to distract us while others escaped. Early on the 8th of July, B Company cleared through Haji Musa encountering a sizeable enemy group.

During this fight, MCpl Harding's section (C/S 23A) was securing the western flank of the village of Haji Musa, with 4 Canadian soldiers and 8 ANA soldiers spread out along the defensive posture while elements of 6 Platoon (C/S 22) conducted a sweep of the village itself. At approximately 0900, 20-30 insurgents attacked the west flank from at least two positions to the north and west of

23A at a distance of approximately 50m. The 8 ANA took cover from the intense RPG and MG fire. MCpl Harding engaged the enemy and then began to try and bring the ANA into the firefight. He repeatedly ran back to grab an ANA soldier and bring him forward to the frontline position, each time at great personal risk. During the firefight, Cpl Klodt was shot in the neck and needed to be evacuated. Upon ordering a withdrawal, the ANA soldiers promptly left, leaving MCpl Harding and the remaining two soldiers of 23A to suppress the numerically superior enemy, conduct first aid while under fire, and evacuate Cpl Klodt to a rally point with elements of C/S 22. They did all this successfully. MCpl Harding's courageous and decisive action under intense enemy fire successfully held the west flank until the injury to Cpl Klodt forced them to withdrawal. His decision to put himself in harm's way in an attempt to bring the ANA into the fight, returning repeatedly to the frontline despite a heavy volume of enemy fire, demonstrated selflessness and gallantry that occurred on many occasions throughout these battles.

In a separate remarkable event to the north in A Company Pte Adams found himself laying 10 feet way from the impact of a 500 lb. bomb. Luckily, soft ground and a low wall channelled the blast away from Adams and he was MEDEVAC-ed out with a mild concussion and damaged eardrum. Cpl Mooney and Sgt Shipway were subsequently wounded in fighting on the C Company front. Some of our casualties were evacuated by helo along with 4 ANA and one Talib through 9er Tac's position, and I was able to see the casualties off, something that made me appreciate more the need for good tactical decision-making, cognizant of the price we would pay for lack of attention on my part. On 9 July, in assaulting one of the last remaining Taliban compounds, Pte Boneca, an excellent reserve soldier from the Lake Superior Scottish Regiment, was killed while conducting close-quarter clearance of a multi-storey structure. The enemy in this complex were few – three in total, but died fighting hard. The toughest was named by our forces as "the man who wouldn't die" for his incredible ability to survive after every type of munition was dropped upon the compound. Eventually a Hellfire missile was employed, which struck what was certainly a large enemy munitions cache, most likely with mines and shells used for making IEDs. The secondary explosions lasted for a long time, and wounded some of our soldiers. The compound was captured and cleared thoroughly. The following day we completed our clearances and exploited south and west; only to discover that the enemy remnants had withdrawn. We then conducted a retrograde operation to Patrol Base Wilson, where we conducted a media event and took stock before preparing to deploy to Helmand as part of Operation Hewad.

Concept of Operations – Finishing the Enemy

Finishing the enemy in close-combat meant killing or capturing them, and then capitalizing upon this act with aggressive information operations intended to reduce enemy confidence and raise that of the local populace (and our citizens back home). We never construed the use of lethal force as a negative action, or a "last resort". By the time that TF Orion came to be engaging enemy forces on a daily basis (in June, July and August), I had stopped thinking about clever ways of winning without fighting. I realized that "shattering enemy cohesion" and maintaining the initiative required a degree of physical destruction. In the emerging discussion of Effects Based Operations I contribute this; the best second-order and third-order effects are produced by first killing some enemy and then using such destruction to best advantage in information operations. In cultures where degrees of violence are largely accepted and indicative of strength, this is how insurgents are beaten. The idea of winning without hard fighting is complete folly. However, the act of destruction only served to finish an enemy group if we ended the action by remaining on the battlefield – forcing him to withdraw – and then beating the enemy to the punch by communicating with the Afghans first, telling them about our successful reduction of enemy fighting power and especially about how the *Dushman* withdrew from the area, conceding our superiority of arms. By this we achieved local (tactical) psychological advantage that allowed us to maintain the operational initiative and to begin to consider re-introducing governance and reconstruction projects. Physical reductions in counter-insurgency are less important than psychological reductions by publicly attacking the enemy's status. But you require both to win. The true finishing of the *Dushman* was achieved each time we reduced the status of a Taliban group to "a has-been" in the eyes of the locals. This we did during large press conferences such as that conducted on 12 July.

Operation Zahar was important in several regards. It destroyed an enemy group that had controlled Pashmul for a month, evicting locals, preparing fortifications and communications routes, and ambushing Highway One. It reinforced our freedom of movement and denied the same to the enemy. It demonstrated to locals our strength and capability. It policed from the battlefield over two hundred large munitions. Most of all it gained time for Kandahar City, increasingly under threat of attack. From a TF perspective the operation confirmed many things. We needed the critical mass of three manoeuvre companies to trap the enemy. In this war, we required considerable massing of forces to destroy even a small number of enemy. Also, the increased number of ANA provided quantum improvement in our capability; they could practically smell the presence of the *Dushman*. A significant improvement also came with the attachment to the TF of a US Army Route Clearance Package, a three-vehicle IED-finding capability that was instrumental in locating three IEDs and saving us from damage and death. The Engineer Squadron Commander, Maj Trevor Webb, personally escorted this superb and extremely vulnerable capability around the battlefield, clearing routes and providing us freedom of movement.

On the negative side, we realized from Operation Zahar that the enemy were still in Zharie/Panjwayi in great strength and that our operations had but temporary effect. What would be required was a long-term operation with an aim to implant ANSF in the district permanently. A prerequisite to this would be the need to convince the Division of the threat, and of the need for sustained operations. While we could find, fix and finish Taliban groups at the tactical level, TF Orion was not big enough to finish the Operational Level insurgency into Zhairie and Panjwayi. This was nagging on our minds as we left B Company alone in Zharie/Panjwayi to continue security operations there, supported by the PRT. We released the UK Household Cavalry Squadron that we had OPCON since July 6th, and in accordance with "the Plan" we set our sights upon Helmand.

Maj Fletcher and I flew to Camp Bastion to liaise with the 3rd Battalion the Parachute Regiment, to whom C Company would be put under operational control for part of Operation Hewad, with a task to support their battalion operations in Sangin, an area well-known to C Company. I would coordinate that support and re-supply, A Company would provide a long-range outer cordon on the mountain passes to the east of Sangin, and A Battery, 9er Tac and Recce Platoon would secure the LOCs south of Sangin to Gereshk and Lashkar Gah. To support us, TF Orion received under operational control D (Devil) Company of 2-4 Infantry (TF Warrior) from Zabul Province, under Capt Steven Wallace.

PHOTO 5:TF Leaguer   Courtesy of John D. McHugh Recce P1 1 PPCLI
150 Vehicles awaiting sandstorm to slip into Helmand

We staged forward toward Helmand and leaguered our forces in the open in Maywand, just off of Highway One, parading 150 vehicles in a show of power for the locals to see and for the Taliban to report on. Part of our task was to put pressure upon the Taliban command and control system throughout Helmand and Kandahar. I therefore wanted them to see and hear of this massive array of combat power preparing to move somewhere unknown to them. I deliberately fed information to certain ANP officers that we might move north to Ghorak and Khakrez districts to dominate those areas in a follow-on operation to Jagra and Tabar. We knew from the enemy's

ICOM chatter and other intelligence that this parading of force was indeed causing them some apprehension. Our next problem was manoeuvring this force westward without totally disclosing our intent.

Our chance came that evening – 12 July – with the arrival of a sandstorm. As it blew in, I knew that this was a perfect chance to infiltrate. We issued fragmentary orders for a rapid move by packets into Helmand. Off of the map I selected a small depression in a patch of desert just south of Heyderabad. We snaked by long columns into this place in the middle of the night as the sandstorm began to wane. For the first time since we had begun operations in February, I knew that the *Dushman* had no idea of our whereabouts. They had always tracked our movements, large and small. That night, they lost us.

When we were secure in our desert leaguer, I summoned OC A Company, (Maj Kirk Gallinger) and the Recce Platoon Commander (Hamilton) and directed that they proceed under darkness to Heyderabad. We had good intelligence of an enemy compound there from which an enemy IED cell operated regularly. They departed immediately, supported by a troop of A Battery, co-located with the leaguer.

Just before first light, this force made contact. The enemy's early warning parties awoke to the probes of Recce Platoon, and hit a recce detachment with RPG, PKM and AK 47 fire. Recce Platoon needed support and they received it immediately, as A Company LAVs arrived beside them to pour intense 25 mm fire into the enemy positions. Together the two forces advanced and cleared the target compound. 14 enemy were killed that morning, including a group leader. IED material, documents, and propaganda were captured (some of the propaganda specifically identifying Canadians as an enemy). Also captured was 3 million dollars (local value) of Opium paste, with a street value 4-5 times that amount. Our forces suffered minor scratches, mainly caused by near misses and bullets

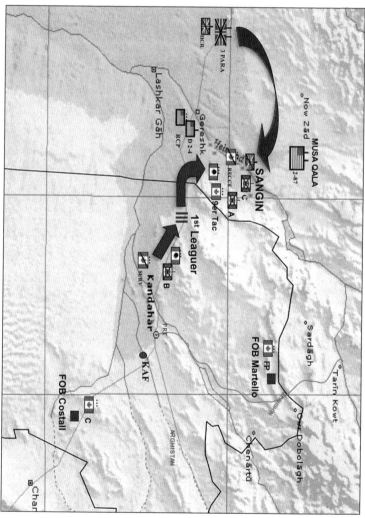

MAP 12: Op HEWAD – Sangin

impacting on armour plating. Sgt Mars Janek was hit this way. Withdrawing from the enemy fire as the LAVs rolled forward, he stopped to physically pick up two soldiers who had stumbled, one in each hand, when he was hit by a 7.62mm round in the back plate. Despite this he remained characteristically quiet, pragmatic, and unperturbed: a true professional.

The morning of 13 July broke clear and hot. We sat in our desert depression preparing for Operation Hewad to commence. As a preliminary we received a task to assist the British platoon in Sangin with re-supply. They were down to their last bottles of water. A British re-supply convoy would linkup with us and be escorted by our C Company to Sangin, with C Company then moving to FOB Robinson to be ready for the insertion of 3 Para on July 15th.

The British convoy arrived at our leaguer and proceeded to dump the supplies for the Sangin troops on the desert floor. They stated that they had orders not to proceed in their relatively unarmed vehicles to Sangin, but to give the supplies to the Canadians for transport. This was unexpected. With wrinkled brows, both OC C Company and I discussed options and it was decided that C Company would leave its own supplies here – to be moved forward by 9er Tac – and take the British supplies into Sangin that day. They unloaded their own stores in order to reload the Brits', and then departed for their task. I was not at all happy with this change of circumstances and fought the uncomfortable feeling that the British would not hesitate to take advantage of Maj Fletcher's combat capability, forcing him to assume risk by conducting tasks that were not articulated in our initial combined planning. This fear was also reinforced by the inadequate planning that was evident that day, when we discovered that no troop coordination measures had been designated, making it difficult for us to plan coordination of fire and manoeuvre between all of our battalions. This increased my conviction to move forward to FOB Robinson in order to exert presence upon any situation that might begin to unravel. While the focus of attention was to be in Sangin District Centre itself, the CO of 3 Para was going to be on the ground there for only one of the five days of operations, the remainder of the time he would be 120 kilometres away in Camp Bastion. I felt that it might be useful to be on hand to exercise influence and control over the incredible massing of forces (three large battalions) that was about to happen.

C Company got to Sangin and delivered the British supplies, the effect of their LAVs again exercising a deterrent upon the violence there. We issued orders that placed part of A Company in cut-off positions by the mountain passes east of Sangin, the remainder of A Company and Recce Platoon between FOB Robinson and Heyderabad, and Devil Company 2-4 Infantry between Heyderabad and Highway One (Gheresk). Both A and D Companies were to keep open the LOCs from FOB Robinson south, to harass enemy along the Helmand River, especially in the Heyderabad district, putting pressure on the Taliban C2 system over a broad front, and prepared to assist 3 Para if required. I moved with the Gun troop to a central position from which the M777 could engage in support all Canadian, UK, and American troops from C company in Sangin, south to D Company on Highway One. Maj Trevor Webb, Engineer Squadron Commander, and Maj Mason Stalker (now in my Tac CP) carried on the difficult but essential task of planning and conducting route clearances in front of all of our supply and reinforcement columns using the US Route Clearance Package. Their efforts found and disabled three more IEDs that would have had a severe negative impact upon our operations. We did our best to ensure that all major convoys were preceded by this clearance capability, making the coordination of all TF movement, handing off this package from one convoy to the next, a considerable planning problem, executed extremely well by Stalker and his staff.

From 14-17 July, A and D company harassed the enemy along the Helmand River south of Sangin, engaging in multiple fire-fights everyday. Their orders were to not become decisively engaged, to avoid getting bogged down in the thick greenbelt that exists on either side of the Helmand, and to avoid casualties. They did this wonderfully, demonstrating excellent control and restraint, yet remaining aggressive. Without a doubt, we retained the operational initiative completely. The ICOM and other intelligence we received confirmed that the enemy in this area was in complete disarray.

On the afternoon of 15 July C Company, after supporting the 3 Para airmobile assault onto north Sangin, was chopped back to us and I attached a platoon of A Company. We were directed by Brigade to conduct BDA in southern Sangin, after a significant air strike on a concentration of enemy. In moving to the strike site, C Company group came into a hard engagement with approximately 100 Taliban, firing from well-dispersed defensive positions across a broad front. This was in a very complex built-up area. After engaging the enemy with multiple support fires, we ordered C Company out of the fight at last light; subsequent combat tasks being more important than this BDA mission. In FOB Robinson we planned for our next phase. The following morning, a very large concentration of forces moved into Sangin in an effort to clear the area around the besieged British compound, secure better re-supply landing zones, and clear the enemy from the town centre. I again chopped C Company to 3 Para, and moved forward to observe the operation from an old

123

Soviet defensive position high above the East of the town. There was some minor skirmishing that day. It became clear that the enemy had departed or had chosen to lay low. We began to plan for retrograde of the entire TF, to commence on the 17th of July. We issued orders that night.

9er Tac would commence the retrograde, moving south of FOB Robinson to work with Recce Platoon to continue harassing patrols along the Helmand River while A, C and D companies conducted re-supply in preparation for phased withdrawal back to KAF on the 18th. D Company in the south were continuing to pressure Heyderabad with combat patrols, and I wanted to visit them to thank then for their excellent support to us before they were to be detached from TF Orion early the next day. As we moved south to linkup with them, they became engaged in a fierce firefight. My convoy was the closest available LAV capability; so what had begun as a visit quickly turned into combat support.

Capt Steven Wallace had his 150-man company of US Army infantry positioned with two platoons facing west, the right flank platoon clearing compounds in the village of Heyderabad. The left platoon was deployed along a narrow ridge with the troops firing into a series of compounds and orchards from which the Taliban had ambushed his forces. Wallace had one HUMVEE damaged by RPG fire inflicting minor shrapnel wounds to one soldier. He was in fine spirits when 9er Tac arrived, happy to be engaging the enemy in a full-blown fight. His company had been under my operational control for seven days now – the first US Army infantry under Canadian control in combat in fifty years. His soldiers had been relegated to economy-of-force tasks, producing only fleeting contact with insurgent fighters. This had frustrated Wallace, who wanted action, and he was very happy as my LAV and that of Maj Steve Gallagher (G19), joined his command vehicle atop the narrow ridge that formed the firing line for his left platoon. He gave me quick target indication and I passed these to my gunner – Cpl Greg Davis – who began to engage Taliban firing positions 100-150 metres to our front. It was approximately 3:30 PM. After only several minutes of our fire the enemy began to withdraw, giving us brief glimpses of dark-turbaned forms running between compound walls and into the "green belt". The compounds from which they had fought were at the edge of the fertile area of green cultivation that lay astride the Helmand River, and comprised a complex of connected and compounded farms and fields and villages, highly compartmentalized and hardly traversable to us because of the narrow roads, high walls, and wide and deep irrigation canals. Its lush green orchards and fields, growing bountiful poppy crops, were stark contrast to the desert that rolled up to its edges. Both Wallace and I knew from a previous fight in this location that once this enemy entered into the green belt he would be able to easily escape. Wallace ordered a platoon to chase the enemy on foot. The US infantryman alighted from their HUMVEES and began to muster in files to assault into the first compound. My LAV provided intimate support, covering their movement with fire and acting as a moving armoured shield to the vulnerable infantrymen as they walked forward. We also attempted to give these soldiers an easy breach into the compound by using our cannon fire to put a hole into the closest wall. The thickness and hardness of the wall prevailed. RSM Randy Northrup dismounted and used a M72 anti-tank weapon to try to produce a hole; nothing. US infantrymen began to grin at our impotence, but gave a cheer when my driver Cpl Stitch Hayward slowly rolled forward and battered a hole in the wall a perfect width for the infantry squads to breach. They ran in. The height of our

LAVs allowed us to maintain visual contact with them as they began searching the compounds and orchards of the enemy fighting positions, finding weaponry, blood trails, and body parts – severed off by Davis' 25mm cannon fire.

We continued to give support to the dismounted American infantry as they cleared from south to north along the western portion of Heyderabad, between the village and a deep canal to the west. Several times they came under intense enemy fire from north and from the west bank of the canal. We used mortars to neutralize the westernmost enemy group, and direct fire from small arms and from our two LAVs to destroy the group to the north. I jockeyed 9er Tac from firing position to firing position on the right flank of the US infantry, engaging the enemy as they attempted to establish ambush lines in front the American infantry, until a point where, when rounding a narrow corner between a compound and a house, we were hit by RPG fire. The first round passed between the cannon and the driver's hatch and struck the wall beside me. It disabled our communications in the turret so that Davis and I could not speak to each other. Stitch reversed a few yards to a position where I could just see over a wall at the enemy's firing positions, but could not communicate a target indication to Davis. A US Army sergeant with two dismounted squads was just behind the LAV asking directions from me. In frustration at the inability to yell to him over the noise of firing, and wanting him to see where the enemy was, I grabbed my rifle (always placed beside me in the bustle rack of the LAV turret) and jumped out of the turret and down behind the LAV. I told the sergeant to follow me and we began in long single file to work our way around the compound on our right – attempting to find a place to flank the enemy. We skirted the compound and entered an open rice field. Once exposed, we came under heavy small arms fire from the same enemy. The US soldiers needed no orders from their platoon leaders or me; they immediately spread out into two squad lines and began to advance and to fire all their weaponry into the enemy. The exchange of fire was about even, but the enemy's passed over our heads whilst ours found the mark. The swift action of the American infantrymen – a result of many hours of battle drills training, and the efficiency of the sergeants (all now four-year veterans with multiple tours in Afghanistan and Iraq) – was very effective. The enemy fire slackened. I was proud of these Devil soldiers. I reflected later upon this, and realized that at some point in the past decade we have had a fundamental shift in the culture of the Canadian infantry, making us identify most readily with American, and not British, infantry. Devil Company was easy to work with, reliable, and very professional. Perhaps the biggest similarity was that they wanted to fight, unlike the soldiers of other allied countries who remained very risk-averse, too shy to stand and fight the Taliban. When firing began, the American leaders demonstrated decisiveness and tenacity, and the American soldiers performed battle drills quickly and with great effect.

At that time a young American platoon commander arrived and took charge of his men. I told him to continue his fire but not to advance forward as I intended to finish the enemy with LAV and artillery fire. He agreed. As I made my way back to the LAVs I attempted to create as small a target as possible to the bullets zipping past and hitting the wall behind me. I heard more RPG fire further west. 9er Tac was still without communications when I returned, so G19 took our place in the firing position. The combined effect of LAV and small fire from two directions forced the enemy to stop and withdraw. Capt Wallace asked if he should attempt to chase the enemy into the green belt. With the oncoming darkness I told him no, but reinforced to him our policy of remaining on the battlefield after each fight until it was clear to both the enemy and to any non-combatants that it was the Taliban and not us that gave ground. Our withdrawal would occur after darkness and after our superiority of arms was made clear to all. Wallace understood this. Maintaining the initiative was as much a psychological matter as anything else. It required a moral ascendancy over the enemy. He busied him-self sorting out his troops and assisting in our attempts to chase the withdrawing enemy with close air support and artillery fire. Two groups of enemy were observed and tracked as they withdrew from Heyderabad and crossed the canal, moving into a fairly prominent yellow building. G19 brought aircraft and artillery onto that target. These were effective, and the target building must have housed a considerable weapons cache, for we could hear and observe the sec-ondary explosions for over an hour after our strike.

I met Wallace as the light was fading, thanked him for his support and service, gave him a TF Orion coin and said good-bye to him. His company was scheduled to be moved back to his parent US bat-talion early the next morning. I was regretting the thought of losing these troops. We gathered the 9er Tac convoy and proceeded on a slow and careful trek back to A Company's position 7 kilometres away, travelling off road and without light to avoid IED and am-bush. We arrived at A Company at 11:00 PM. I was exhausted. We had been on the go since 04:00 AM and the post-combat adrena-lin slide was occurring. I questioned my Operations Officer – Maj Stalker – whether or not we were ready to begin retrograde move-ments back to KAF the following day. He assured me that the orders and been sent and acknowledged and that he would coordinate the rest. This was welcome news as I felt the need for deep and pro-longed sleep. I went back to 9er Tac to find – characteristically –

the boys already snoring, and the back ramp down and the bench ready for me to curl up upon with a folded raincoat for a pillow and a ranger blanket to ward off early morning chill. I had just finished loosening the laces on my boots (we slept fully clothed but you need to loosen belts and laces to allow circulation, otherwise you will be awakened by pain) and was on the brink of instantaneous sleep, when a duty officer climbed onto the back ramp and informed me that the brigade commander would give me radio orders in five minutes. Shaking the cobwebs from my brain I walked blurry-eyed to the command post.

The tactical command post was a 16x24 foot rough tent attached to the back of a Bison armoured vehicle and contained three radio sets on tables, satellite (SAT) phones, a satellite laptop, a map table and chairs, and – thank God – a coffee pot always full. I sat by the command radio and after a few minutes heard the brigade commander's voice. Receiving radio orders was a rare occurrence – I knew that something important was happening because I could not remember such an occurrence. Normally the brigade commander approved our concept of operations plan before an operation commenced and we got on with it. Obviously we were about to receive new tasks that were important, and I knew we could forget about going back to KAF for a shower. The brigade commander came on and relayed to me that the District Centres in Nawa and Garmser had fallen to the enemy that day. President Karzai was very concerned, as were the US and British commanders and the Governor of Helmand. It was surmised that the Taliban were deliberately moving onto Lashkar Gah in an effort to stop our operations in Sangin. Lashkar Gah was exposed. TF Orion was ordered to retake the Nawa and Garmser District Centres by 4:30 PM the next day. "Are there any questions?" "Roger Sir", I said, "Just one. Where are Nawa and Garmser?" The brigade commander responded in the tone conveying understanding; "they are in southern Helmand," he said. "Roger," I said. "But we have no maps". The following silence also conveyed his understanding; without maps it would be impossible to do the task; and the production and distribution of maps for a whole TF would take hours. "We will get maps to you as soon as possible" said the brigadier. I then knew we had hours to prepare in-place before we could move. Helicopters were ordered to bring maps to us by first light, and a helicopter would also come to take my command team on a reconnaissance at first light. There was obvious tension after the radio orders were over, as everyone knew that we were staying out in the heat and dust and danger for another week; it had already been 11 days. We had manoeuvred over 350 kilometres and fought in over 20 intense firefights. We had rescued the beleaguered British garrison in Sangin and continuously put pressure upon the Taliban over a frontage of 70 kilometres. The sentiment was "isn't there anyone else they can task to do their hard work...we are tired of rescuing everyone". This normally "cando" organization was feeling very victimized. I gathered a few key folks and told them to get over it, this was obviously very serious and good people were looking at all the options – and that these good people had determined that we were the best option. I then had to deliver more bad news to Mason Stalker. While I would normally have given the bad news to the company commanders, I needed him to relay the warning order to them by radio and do some planning to concentrate our three companies (dispersed over the 70 kilometres) for orders and to organize re-supply for us before we advanced south toward Nawa and Garmser. I told him that I was going to bed, I needed sleep. I was still overcoming the post adrenalin rush and the brush with death. I knew that we were in for a longer haul, and that as a commander I needed to be "in the zone" when making decisions in the next few days. So I went back to my bench and fell into deep sleep.

I awoke prior to first-light at just past 4:00 AM and tightened my boots and went looking for a coffee. The maps had not yet arrived when the reconnaissance helicopter was inbound. A Company Commander, Gallinger, and I jumped aboard and asked if maps were in the bird. The aircrew had only aerial maps, but they did inform us that Nawa and Garmser were south of Lashkar Gah on the Helmand River. Further complicating matters was the fact that the headsets on the helo were not working, and I was the only one able to communicate with the pilots. Kirk sat behind me without a map and without sound, basically a passenger. We flew to pick up Wallace and I was happy that he was ordered to stay with us for the next phase. His smile as he boarded the bird revealed his mutual satisfaction at staying. He liked working for an organization that let him fight. We proceeded south.

Without a map and with no real knowledge of where Nawa and Garmser were, I took out pencil and paper and began to sketch our routes. I had been to Lashkar Gah before and knew that much of the journey. From Lash we would have to proceed south following the southerly flow of the wide Helmand River. On either side of the river stretched 3-5 kilometres of farmland and village, with a maze of roads and trails winding between them. I told the pilots I needed two routes traversable to LAVs and heavy vehicles. I watched the main roads and the prominent tracks and tried to memorize details of major intersections and chokepoints – then quickly sketch them. Several times I had to ask the pilots to turn around when I saw a track I was following disappear into nothing and we would backtrack to find an alternate route. We then flew over the Nawa

District Centre – 30 kilometres south of Lashkar Gah. The villages were empty – meaning that the Taliban were present. Garmser (60 kilometres further south) was the same, but harder. It was on the east bank of the Helmand, and we had to approach from the west. There was only one bridge over Helmand south of Lash, at

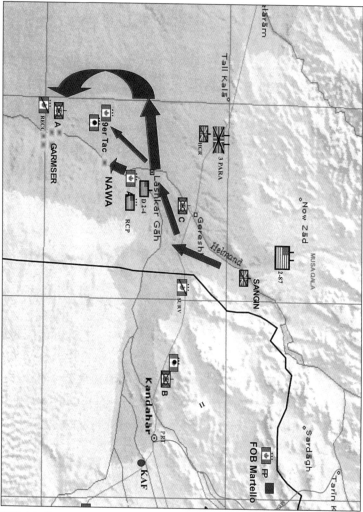

MAP 13: Nawa-Garmser

Garmser, and it was 500 metres long, single lane and was 30 feet over the river and very vulnerable to fire if we attempted to cross in the face of the enemy. I had no doubt that the enemy were present in the otherwise empty town.

We had no maps, and only sparse intelligence of the enemy. We received a grainy air photo of each of the district centres and a half-page written report and hand drawn sketch of Garmser. This, coupled with my hand-drawn sketch of the two routes we would take, was something very much less than I expected in modern warfare in 2006. But I was confident. We returned to the Task Force and all of the companies began to muster together – 150 vehicles – to re-supply and to conduct a brief "face-to-face" before starting. I found WO Armstrong and the Tactical Command Post with maps, and we taped together a number of sets and I took a yellow highlighter and traced the routes on the map from my sketch and then gathered the company commanders together for quick orders. These lasted about fifteen minutes, after which I despatched Kirk (with Recce Platoon attached) first on the long route that would take him over 120 kilometres from our location, well west into the desert area southwest of Lashkar Gah and then south and east toward Garmser. This allowed them to circumvent Nawa and the thickest part of the green belt, and hopefully the Taliban would report this movement and their forces in Nawa would start to panic about being flanked. I then wanted Devil Company to go straight south from Lash to Nawa, with 1 Platoon A Company attached to give them a LAV vanguard. I would go between the forces, accompanying the artillery and ensuring that our guns were in range of both forces at all times. I had arranged to stop just west of Lashkar Gah – on the west end of the bridge over the Helmand River – to meet with the Helmand Deputy Governor, Provincial Police Chief and liaison officers from UK forces. We conferred for 30 minutes. They provided good information, confirmed the substantial fear in Lashkar Gah about the possible Taliban attack, and offered approximately 100 ANP to support our operations. I divided these police between our companies, agreeing to escort those dedicated to A Company (already moving south) and deliver them that day to Gallinger. Wallace took his ANP undertow. Bill Fletcher's C Company organized themselves in Lashkar Gah to protect the UK PRT and the town, and to be prepared to escort our re-supply convoys when they came. I then proceeded west in pursuit of A Company as Devil Company (with Capt Kevin Schamuhn's 1 Platoon leading) proceeded due south on the west bank of the Helmand River. It was past noon hour and we had only a few hours left.

Nawa District Centre has fallen. The governor has fled to Lashkar Gah. Anywhere south should be assumed to be in TB hands, either through re-negotiation or force.

The next phase could see an attack on a 'British' base at the mouth of the Helmand River (pass called Kala Bust) and, at the same time, an attack against the Bolan Bridge (SW of Lash).

If these are successfully a four pronged attack against Lashkar Gah will be launched IOT take the city.

POC Maj ████████████

J2 AEGIS

— 2000Z - NAWA D.C. on fire.

DIAGRAM 3: Intel of Nawa-Garmser

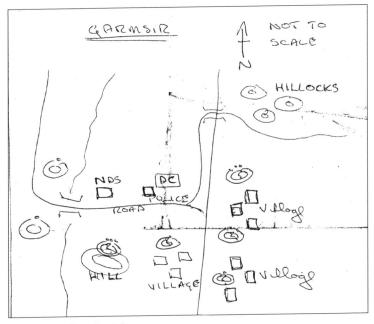

DIAGRAM 4: Sketch of Garmser

By 4:30 PM Kevin Schamuhn's platoon and Devil Company stormed into Nawa unobstructed. There was minor skirmishing and IED finds that day and the next, but the enemy had clearly evacuated in the wake of the A Company's western flank manoeuvre and before D Company's advance. By 4:30 PM, A Company was on the west bank of the Helmand across from Garmser ready to assault across the bridge into the District Centre. The enemy was present in strength, firing dozens of RPGs across the river at at our forces. Kirk Gallagher would have proceeded but for two delaying events. We had a vehicle breakdown with the artillery troop that was to support his fight and at 4:30 PM we were still out of range to provide the needed fire support; also, locals had informed him that the Taliban had mined the narrow bridge, and it would be very difficult to find and clear these mines after dark. In radio discussions with Kirk we agreed to wait until first light to attack. Once our vehicle problem was sorted (the Canadian soldier is a master a improvising vehicle repairs and recovery) we proceeded to establish an artillery Gun Position at a location that could provide best support to both A and D Companies and to protect our re-supply routes and from which we could coordinate the transfer of casualties and detainees. We were set by 6:30 PM and began to fire in support of A Company, who spent the entire night firing at groups of enemy on the east bank; Taliban fighters who were unfamiliar with the night-firing capability, accuracy, and penetrating power of LAV 25mm cannon rounds.

By first light Kirk's company and Recce Platoon were advancing into Garmser. A Company skirmished all the way through the town, forcing the Taliban out block-by-block. Kirk maintained a very deliberate and balanced approach, never extending his soldiers so that small groups could be isolated, ambushed, and cut off. Instead he always presented a powerful front to the enemy, so that they could not hope to ambush anyone and survive. Because of this A Company suffered no casualties, inflicted dozens, and broke the enemy's resolve to defend Garmser. By 8:30 AM, A Company owned the empty town. I arrived shortly after that to deliver about 40 ANP and the Provincial Chief of Police and Deputy Governor, who were determined to stay there and establish government presence in Garmser once again. Kirk met them and I gave them an Afghan national flag to hoist above the District Centre. This they did, to the satisfaction of A Company and Recce Platoon soldiers, who knew they had achieved something special.

Our forces stayed in the Nawa and Garmser districts for the next four days until UK and ANA forces were sent to relieve us. In that time, there were over fifteen substantial firefights with the enemy as A Company continued to push the security bubble further east and south. At that time A Company was fighting at the end of a 240 kilometre supply chain overland from KAF. This required a daily drop-off of ammo, water and fuel. Never did we want for any of these commodities, largely due to the personal efforts of LCol John Conrad and to our excellent staffs. The dedicated folks in our Maintenance, Supply, and Transport platoons performed yeoman service for days on end, without sleep, to keep our forces fighting, and endured bad weather, worse roads, and several terrible Taliban ambushes in order to keep us supplied.

On 22 July we handed Garmser and Nawa over to UK forces and ANA/ANP and proceeded to move incrementally back to KAF. I knew we had achieved a great thing and was determined to inform the soldiers. I mustered what I could of A Company and C Company, the guns and the NSE in a field in Helmand, to personally inform the troops of their achievements. I requested a media reception for their arrival back at KAF. I desired to get into the press some coverage of their remarkable feat-of-arms, very much overshadowed in the news cycle by events in Lebanon, but no less deserving of coverage. I wanted to gloat to the Taliban about our superiority in fighting. I wanted to let Afghans know that we were here to do whatever was needed to give them a chance at a secure future. All my wishes were moot when I received the radio message – while driving into KAF – that our support convoy was hit by a Suicide IED in western Kandahar City enroute back to KAF. Dead were Cpls Francisco Gomez and Jason Warren, and 10 others were injured. I spent the night in the hospital and writing letters. My initial instinct was to avoid the press conference scheduled for the following morning. But I came to realize that night that it would not be wrong to explain the operations. The achievements were indeed overshadowed by our late losses. But I knew Gomez (we had been in the Airborne Regiment together); he and Warren would want Canadians to know what TF Orion had achieved for Canada and for the Afghan people. It was a story I told with solemnity. I reflected many times that night that this indeed was "The Long War".

In late July and early August, we were in contact with the *Dushman* everyday. On the 9th of August TF Orion began to handover responsibility for Kandahar to the TF 3-06, a relief-in-place in contact that lasted 10 days. This was a difficult task, as it was clear that the Taliban were still attempting to consolidate in Zharie/Panjwayi with designs on Kandahar City. We were now being told that it was their stated aim was not just to conduct a spectacular (Tet Offensive style) attack, but to capture the city permanently by autumn. They wanted to launch substantial attacks onto Kandahar city on the weekend celebration of Afghan Independence Day – 19 August. However, aggressive TF Orion actions between 02-11 August preempted this by reducing their combat capacity and thereby buying time for the planning of larger – brigade-size – operations aimed at eliminating the Taliban in Zharie/Panjwayi (Operation Medusa). However, this operation could not begin before September, and during the intervening time there was – at best – a standoff in those districts, and at times the Taliban held the initiative, with superiority of forces and freedom of movement. I toured the area of operations in these contested districts on August 16th and 17th. Within 30 minutes of arriving at the Zharie District Centre we were under severe mortar attack. It was the baptism of fire for the new sub-unit there – A Company of 2 PPCLI. The mortar fire injured six soldiers and it fell to myself and my RSM to mentor the newcomers on how to collect and administer casualties, complete 9-liner radio messages, and organize the helicopter MEDEVAC. Meanwhile my

Battery Commander – Maj Steve Gallagher – led A Company out of the base to take the fight to the enemy, supporting OC A – Maj Mike Wright. A Company's injuries were minor, and this proved to be a shocking but necessary inoculation to their new environment.

PHOTO 6: Breakfast with the ANA – Panjwayi, 17 Aug (Handing over the AO to LCol Lavoie – 3rd from right)

Courtesy of Author

That night I once again made the careful nocturnal move to Panjwayi District Centre – arriving at first light to discover – with impression – that the ANA and ANP were there conducting a co-ordinated defence of the town. This was a first – normally these organizations worked poorly together. Equally impressive was the fact that the ANA were there without any ETT. These Afghan soldiers, under the leadership of an old veteran ANA major – veteran of several older Afghan wars, were independently defending this critical gateway to Kandahar City. Also there, was my friend and comrade Capt Massoud, living in trench on a small hill above Panjwayi. I asked why he was out here alone, to hear him reply that if he did not stay here himself, his fighters would desert. I reflected that leadership principles were universal. Only through shared risk and hardship could fighting spirit be maintained. I loved this man and felt very strongly about the fact that I could not stay out there with him at this critical time. I was disturbed by their news of Taliban activity; nightly probes and a brazen manner that would not be contemplated if LAVs were with them. I promptly directed A Company to deploy a platoon to assist with the defence of Panjwayi. Maj Mike Wright and one platoon came the next day, just in time to prevent the town from falling into enemy hands.

On the 19th of August, Afghan Independence Day, the Afghan authorities held festive celebrations in Kandahar City. I deployed in charge of ISAF security there, but remained worried about the situation on Panjwayi. That night the battle commenced. An estimated 400 enemy fighters began a comprehensive encirclement of the town. Their aim was clear – to demonstrate to the world their potency during the national celebration. Their desire to attack Kandahar City was thwarted by our actions on August 3rd, so they instead wanted to seize a major district centre only 15 kilometres from Kandahar City – showing their power and potential. Maj Wright and his A Company platoon were present for the initial fight, but were not adequately forewarned regarding the intensity of the enemy attack. After an hour of severe exchanges of fire they were forced to withdraw from the battle area to standoff positions to the east. I was no longer in command of the AO, yet I was desperate that the District Centre not fall, which would be a travesty at the end of our hard-fought tour. I requested that A Company be pushed back into the fight and asked the Brigade to release authority to apply all available fire support in support of the beleaguered ANA and ANP fighters – who were sustaining casualties. I then personally went to the US armed UAV control centre to coordinate missile fire in support of our troops. I worried for the fate of Maj Ahmed – the ANA commander – and especially for my friend Capt Massoud. However, substantial artillery and US air bombing support turned the tide and broke up the Taliban attacks. The re-entrance of A Company into the fight finalized the defensive battle and the Taliban withdrew with over 50 casualties. While some media portrayed this action as a well-planned deliberate fight orchestrated by ISAF HQs, the reality was that it was a series of desperate and unplanned hard-fought actions by front line soldiers against a coherent enemy offensive. The net result was to buy needed time for the proper preparation of the brigade attack that was to commence 14 days later. It achieved that. After much concern on the night of the 19th of August, we relaxed the next day and spent the final four days of the tour travelling around and verbally preparing Afghan and Canadians alike to steel themselves for the fight to come. I was the last man of TF Orion to return to KAF on 21 August and I left on the night of the 23rd of August, after a Ramp Ceremony for Cpl Braun, killed in an IED attack in Kandahar City. My parting words to the OC and CSM of A Company were sincere; their soldiers would sustain every hardship imaginable – including all of the intense fighting of the first week of their tour – provided that the OC and CSM stood up to the fear and the danger. Should these leaders falter, the men would be irreversibly reduced. Everything rested upon the shoulders of these two leaders until the brigade arrived. This was the vital lesson – relearned – during our tour; the entire operation ebbed and flowed according to a commander's own personal impulses. The companies were quite content to leaguer up in one area, refitting and attempting to re-set sleep patterns. They were happy to organize themselves around one piece of terrain and establish routine, even though it led to boredom, or even danger, and denied us the initiative. So, commanders had to keep the men moving. Military history does not define for us very well what it really means to seize and maintain the initiative. Yet in Afghanistan this is the single most important thing in defeating the *Dushman*. TF Orion strove to keep him guessing as to our next move, our next objective. We attempted at all time to retain surprise. This was achieved by constant manoeuvre and deception. The leadership of A Company 2 PPCLI, carried this on, striving through force of personality to hold the Taliban at check by continuous activity until Operation Medusa commenced in September. The superbly professional 1st Royal Canadian Regiment Battle Group, under the leadership of LCol Omer Lavoie, supported by UK, Dutch and US forces, then set out to finish the enemy massing in Zharie/Panjwayi, according to official CENTCOM* reports – inflicting 300 enemy killed and another 275 wounded. By then TF Orion was long gone.

---

* CENTCOM: United States Central Command.

Conclusion – The Command Imperatives

Know the War You are in

PHOTO 7: Counter-Insurgency
(AAM Bransfield in Pada Showali Kot)

Courtesy of Major Steve Gallagher

I have not recounted the efforts of the PRT along the governance and security lines of operations. While fraught with inertia and friction, they were more important to the long-term efforts in the Kandahar fight than our military activity. But they could gain no traction while the enemy threatened Kandahar City. I struggled throughout the tour to make people realize the threat posed by the Taliban build up in Kandahar, and to force upon them the understanding that military decision was impossible, that the idea of purely "kinetic" operations was simple-minded, and that to wait for "intelligence-driven" operational planning would lead to inactivity and wasted effort. This was a counter-insurgency operation, not a war of attrition against a military organization, and not simply a counter-terrorist conflict. At stake, every day and in every action, was the confidence of the people. Our military efforts to find, fix, and finish (physically and morally) Taliban groups, were all aimed at increasing local confidence and the more strategic "public will" at home. Only after the tour was over did I see signs of a more general understanding of this. Counter-insurgency requires a complex mix of tasks that include intense combat, as well as massive social and economic reform initiatives. How and when the emphasis shifts from one to the other must involve highly localized decision-making, and decentralizing of the combat function is essential. I believe that the leaders of TF Orion began to know this intuitively by the end of our tour, and this knowledge will serve them well when they command again in tours to come. They will know the war they are in.

Place Personality Above All Else

PHOTO 8: Soldiers in Combat Contact in Pashmul, July 2006   Courtesy of Combat Camera

In garrison in Canada, units can go on for long periods of time without personal supervision of a commanding officer. Our administrative procedures and standard training scenarios make the role of commanding officer, and OC, relatively easy. I felt that I could give broad guidance and leave my battalion in Edmonton for months and feel confident that the unit would carry on quite well in my absence. Even in pre-deployment training, the scenarios presented were never so bad that the soldiers and company leadership could not solve them. I was seldom, if ever, looked to for solutions during garrison routine or on collective training. That is how good "a force generation Army" we have become. None of this adequately prepared us for what we faced in Afghanistan, where the essential moment of combat leadership occurred when soldiers could not conceive of solutions to problems during close combat and turned to us for help. In those moments commanders discovered the true value of being present – not watching on a screen from afar – to find the solution and demonstrate the strength of will needed to bring everyone to that solution collectively. It was at those moments when we discovered the value of years and years of training, professional development, education, and physical conditioning were important. It was there that I saw that not all leaders are equal, and that determination and intellect are the first requirements of command, not nice-to-haves.

In preparation for Afghanistan I worked hard with RSM Northrup to get one thing right, that we select the right command teams from section to sub-unit level, on firm belief that personality and character of leadership was more important than anything else. This emphasis was affirmed in Afghanistan. After our first trials in combat, once we had settled down from first excitements, I trusted in the subordinate commanders because they had natural tenacity and robustness. I trusted that they would not succumb to their fears, but would combine their talent with the natural fighters under their command to enable the platoon or sub-unit to sustain and advance in the midst of chaos, violence, uncertainty and fear to fix and finish the enemy. I trusted that they would learn from mistakes and successes alike, that they would handle death and loss quickly, with dignity, and then move on. I trusted that they would enforce good discipline and order, and yet exercise forgiveness and compassion, without jeopardizing trust and lapsing into blames. All of these trusts combined produced the climate of mission command necessary to winning a counter-insurgency. None of it required sophisticated technologies. The emphasis the Canadian Army placed upon "big head, small-body", "intelligence-driven", "command-centric" operations disappeared in the lush green and highly compartmentalized terrain of Zharie/Panjwayi where good leadership based upon intellect, imagination, experience, determination and trust produced the effective destruction of the enemy. Above all it was the constituent elements of trust that won.

To sustain a unit in prolonged combat there must be a great deal of hierarchical trust, based upon mutual respect of personality. That trust demands understanding and forgiveness; especially when it is clear that fear is visiting. I did not question any request by a subordinate commander who asked for a long water break, or who needed time to sort out communications issues before or during battles. Sometimes I, or one of my subordinate commanders, needed a moment to thrash the dark angel that had chosen that moment to visit, before picking up and carrying on. I knew that commanders were sometimes dealing with battles within themselves, but I never asked the embarrassing questions. To let a man know face-to-face that you see fear in him is to forever compromise him to you. To let his subordinates know that you have seen fear in their commander would spread the fear far. Better to grant him time to deal with it and make it clear that you expect action consistent with the maintenance of the initiative over the enemy. With time most of us became familiar with the violence and uncertainty to a point where right-brain control (rational thinking) combined with fierce determination could win over fear. But it takes time and exposure to come to this point; and trust and understanding and patience are applicable in learning to fight.

If a soldier or leader was known to many to have faltered in combat from fear, there was only one recourse. The commanding officer, if he has any trust left at all, must place this individual beside him, in his crew, and prove to the collective that he is being granted a chance to redeem. He will not let you down.

TF Orion suffered 10% casualties over the course of six and a half months. Loss became familiar. Dealing with loss became a leadership challenge and the most important part of the leadership personality that I observed. The Canadian military has had a fragile nature regarding loss of life. A casualty during a peacekeeping operation would trigger widespread grief within units, and regimental history and memory focused upon dates and places of individual loss – even when attributable to accident. Raising the profile of loss to near-cult status had created a culture hard-pressed to deal with reality of sustained combat. We had to teach ourselves to be harder, to grant the moment for the fallen, but to move on rapidly. Wallowing would not do. Difficult as this was for the soldier, it was harder for the commander. While the privates would mull over their two or three dead friends, I had to deal with them all. It took a great deal of rational thinking (studying the context within which each death occurred) and determination to handle this and to move on; especially if one cares deeply for each life and limb. It is in dealing with loss that Field Marshall Wavell's assertion takes full meaning; the most essential quality of command in war is robustness, a solidness of mind and spirit to the shocks of war and the grief of loss. This must become well understood to commanders entering theatres of war.

Moral Purpose and Decision-making and the Combat Leader

The knowledge that the commanders of TF Orion wanted the soldiers to fight, and by destruction to win, was fundamental to troop morale. Over time, the soldiers came to know that their commanders were constantly looking for enemy for them to kill or capture, and had trust in their ability to do just that. For instance, during the period of April-May, A Coy had the misfortune of operating in the mountains of Showali-kot, where the enemy avoided contact, but made maximum use of IEDs. Morale in A Coy was affected. To reverse this, and to demonstrate trust in the company, I ordered them into the fight in Zharie/Panjwayi and Helmand in July, where they demonstrated their proficiency in arms, and where they exacted retribution upon the Taliban. Their morale soared. They affirmed their professional status, individually as *homo furens* – fighting man; and collectively as a cohesive fighting organization. They gained moral ascendency over the enemy.

PHOTO 9: Shared Risk
(9er Tac LAV after IED strike)

Courtesy of Cpl "Stitch" Hayward - Driver 9er Tac

TF Orion operated under the principles of mission command. Most often the companies operated independently, with 9er Tac moving between them fulfilling coordination functions. During firefights, my job was to work with each sub-unit commander to resource and coordinate fire and manoeuvre, apply air support and intelligence support, exercise liaison with ANSF, and control the evacuation of casualties and prisoners. Exercising direct control over the coordination of supporting functions allowed the subordinate commanders to get on with the brutal business of close-quarter fighting. I trusted and relied upon these commanders to apply the determination, fierceness, and courage that this hard task required. In turn, the junior leaders could rely upon their superiors to provide the best coordination of support. TF Orion applied many dozens of support fires – sometimes at danger close – without blue-on-blue casualties (except Pte Adam, mild concussion) because of the active work of all commanders in controlling the fight. Frequently, companies would fight disparate engagements. At the point of highest tempo in July, the TF fought simultaneously in dispersed operations in Panjwayi, Sangin, and Hyderabad, then Panjwayi, Nawa and Garmser (each company fighting 50-100 kilometres from the others). Solid sub-unit leadership, supported by effective operational coordination by an outstanding battle group staff, handled all these separate fights. At no point in this period of prolonged dispersed combat did I have knowledge of the tactical situation in each sub-unit fight, nor did I need it; because I trusted each sub-unit to continue to execute our concept of offensive manoeuvre operations designed to reduce enemy capacity, maintain the initiative, and continuously create conditions that I could exploit positively in information operations.

This is not to say that I did not expect mistakes to be made. All the commanders of TF Orion made mistakes in operations; mostly because the experience of sustained combat operations was new to us and we had no paradigm or experiential guides. Tactical errors were made by me, and others, that cost life and limb. We who were responsible for these decisions and who gave these orders had to deal with that knowledge immediately – in the face of continued operational pressures – without compromising the faith and trust necessary for mission command to continue to work. TF Orion instituted learning processes to capture lessons learned after each major engagement and to disseminate these throughout the AO. For my part, I emphasized use of the AAR at all levels, sometimes running them myself, in the field, after the fighting was over.

In all of this we did not dwell upon mistakes. Sometimes we did not even speak of them. Nothing is more damaging to trust and self-confidence than to have a man who acted decisively in combat, but had been victim to bad luck, be interrogated by a commander who was not present and had not felt the pressures and complexities of that moment. While I desired that commanders determine quickly what had gone right and what had gone wrong, I did not want this to create an environment of blame. Dealing with loss was a powerful enough motivator to quick learning. Finding quick forgiveness of one another went a long way to avoiding the trap of blame games.

Hierarchical trust was essential to total task force cohesion. It became silently understood that trust and cohesion required an equitable sharing of risk. I travelled everywhere by vehicle, and slept on the ground, and avoided using helicopters because of the impression this left upon the troops. Instead, I would personally lead all road moves until the point where I felt we would begin a final advance to contact. It is my philosophy that the commanding officer must command the lead vehicle, must navigate and make the tactical decisions during all phases of movement. This served several purposes; it relieved a subordinate commander of the additional task of route navigation prior to a battle (allowing him to focus on the close fight after he was delivered to it); it took advantage of the most experienced crew in the BG – my 9er Tac traveled over 9,700 km during the tour and knew the routes and terrain better than any other crew; and this helped avoid unnecessary navigation errors and personal embarrassments to junior leaders who needed their confidence intact before going into battle; and it demonstrated a sharing of risk. The approach came with cost; 9er Tac LAV was hit four times by IEDs and RPGs, resulting in the loss of two of my crew, MCpls Loewen and White, grievously injured on separate occasions by shrapnel. This demonstration of shared risk went far beyond any authority granted by rank and appointment to promote trusts essential to the fighting spirit of TF Orion. It earned us moral authority. The company commanders were always seen well forward in the fighting. They were entrusted to personally lead the close-quarter fight, and to assist me in my role of coordinator of the close battle.

Risk of injury or death was shared, and I, and the sub-unit commanders, came to know intimately the fears of moving across that imaginary line that separates what constituted safe ground and what we knew to be a dangerous place. We came to understand why soldiers kissed their personal talismans before a fight, the fatalistic acceptance of death, how to deal with that visiting shadow that popped the dreaded question in my head "will I ever see my children again?"; and how to dismiss fears and carry on with our tasks. These psychological oscillations are never present in peacetime training; they were the constant companions of those who lived out-of-the-wire, and mark them permanently from those whose relative safety precluded having to deal with that dark shadow. What most visiting officers failed to grasp when talking with our soldiers was that the soldiers had began to judge their leaders by how much personal risk they were prepared to assume. Helicopter "drive by" visits by senior leadership who departed to go and sleep in comfortable places never left any impression upon the soldiers. On the other hand: having a general sleep on the ground beside them, in a dangerous place, won trust immediately. Similarly, soldiers begrudged the imposition of Canadian garrison managerial techniques and regulations when they were enduring the antithesis in an austere and dangerous environment. This extended to regulations prohibiting the wearing of sunglasses on the forehead for even brief periods. The only way to reduce this type of chicken-shit was to spend time with the soldier in their environment, to understand what rules and procedures would have to be modified if we were to keep morale and cohesion. The commanders who spent any time in the field began to understand that to have these soldiers respond right in a fight meant being present – up front – and demonstrating that rank made no one immune from the awful consequences of combat. Shared risk and understanding are essential in establishing hierarchical trusts.

Finally, I must also submit that good combat leadership has a moral foundation that is essential to the profession of arms. I came to realize throughout the period of sustained combat that I had clear moral choices in almost every decision. Decision-making could be either career consequence-based, or based upon moral imperative. Career consequential decision-making had me consider the impact of my decisions upon my career, or the careers and reputations of others. Moral imperative-based decision-making employed moral reasoning skills that considered what was needed tactically at that moment, what was morally allowed with regard to the ROE and laws of war, and what my subordinates needed from me as a leader. Career consequence-based decisions led to safe and cautious courses of action, while moral imperative-based decisions always seemed fraught with risk and tension. As time went on, I found that the moral imperative-based approach was my default.

We needed to make up for lack of numbers by being constantly aggressive and dynamic. I and my staff fought vociferously and hard to try to secure every conceivable ounce of support (AH, UAV, CAS, ANA, etc) for these continuous offensive TF operations, and we aggravated many people with our constant demands. To us, these people did not seem to feel appreciation for our frustration at wanting to conduct continuous aggressive offensive operations, and our sadness at not having enablers and support for the soldiers we were ordering into very complex terrain, outnumbered and outgunned by the Taliban. Our operations were conducted, for the most part, without enablers, and this made us sore. It seemed that too few grasped that we were not winning in Zharie/Panjwayi, and that we could well lose; that we needed to be aggressive to keep the initiative; and that we were under-resourced. I never felt that superiors understood what it was like to order subordinates into certain danger without any support other than our own artillery. I hardened morally from this experience.

My appreciation for moral foundations rose as I witnessed the actions of several higher staff officers: some were afraid to argue on our behalf because it would "rock the boat"; officers from various nations who ordered operations and visits simultaneously, simply so that they could practice war-tourism and claim that they were once "in a battle"; others were quick to express to superiors that our soldiers were "whiners" because we constantly demanded more support. These were not unethical actions. The ethical officer knows the difference and understands that shirking, posturing, and blaming are wrong. The moral officer does not know such distinctions and never shirks, postures, or blames. You can be ethical and careerist at the same time. Moral imperative-based decision-making allowed me to distinguish these things very clearly. Not all commanders and staff officers in war are equal, and careerism and politics are alive and well in combat operations. This understanding left me with an acute sense of being alone. The telling silence from Canada between April and July suggested discomfort in our moral imperative-based choices. The visit of a senior Canadian general in mid-July affirmed this. Tired and pressured from 7 days of combat – with 8 killed and wounded – I received this officer only to hear him wave off my battle briefing and instead proceed to tell me about the image problem that I and TF Orion was having on KAF. I felt betrayed. I also witnessed how completely divorced this officer was from experience of command in danger, with all its moral dilemmas. Subordinate commanders need to hear two things from a visiting superior: "how is it going in your assessment?" and "what do you need from me?" Instead I received a lecture on how to stay in the good graces of higher staffs; a very garrison Canadian approach. I later witnessed this general many times recounting to others of his "being under fire" in the Balkans, a telling attempt to gain credibility and respect from those he had previously claimed were "whiners". From this experience, I realized how careerism and deep-seated inferiority complexes can obliterate moral reasoning. In contrast, the visit of Commander of CEFCOM (Canadian Expeditionary Force Command) in early July was excellent; he personally reassured us that TF Orion was indeed doing well, and upon hearing of our needs he immediately worked to push more resources to us.

Despite the impression of being misunderstood, we carried on as we had started. From May to August all decisions were made based upon moral principles and, as a commander, I lived totally in the very lonely present. I believe this allowed me to focus better on providing the superb men and women under my command the best leadership that I could muster, often failing as it was. Later on, in the post-combat rationalizations that naturally occur, I began to understand that moral reasoning in combat is everything, and must become the foundation of combat command. Careerism, manifest in the Canadian Forces cult of command, rewarding the favourite obedient (regardless of performance), the cookie cutter approach to appointments, the automatic deference to rank, the subordination of soldier needs to politically correct trends, fear of "rocking the boat", indecision for fear of consequences to career, the gratuitous lavishing of awards, and assumed loyalty, are all antithetical of moral reasoning. These careerist trappings may well be the biggest threat we face in transitioning from a garrison army to an army at war. I say this not because we are in bad shape – but because we need to be better. My single biggest learning experience was that good combat leadership needs the strongest moral presence and commitment. Canadian soldiers expect and deserve nothing less.

Epilogue

This account has attempted to relay to the reader my reflections on commanding a fighting organization in a combat environment. I do not pre-suppose that everything I experienced during this fighting has universal application, or was correct in all ways. I know that I have stated many things that stand out like figure eleven targets to some readers, ready to apply their fire. But I hold with unbreakable conviction the underlying theme of this account; which is simply this: a commander's understanding of war, personality, and leadership skill become, above all other things, the critical determinants in battle. They meld together within him or her to form the heart and brain of the fighting organization. When extreme violence, chaos, thirst, and fear combine to crush individual and collective resolve, one thing alone can see the task through – the power of the personality of the section, platoon, company, and battalion commander. Of all other factors in war, none is so decisive. To those who wish to succeed in battle, study the full spectrum of war theory and practice; perfect technical skills; practice moral courage; study hard the ethics of the profession and observe closely the leaders above and around you in order to distinguish between careerist impulses and moral reasoning in command; and harden your emotional disposition without losing compassion for your charges. Prepare these things well and you will be ready when your time comes in the Long War.

Glossary of Acronyms and Abbreviations

2IC	Second-in-Command
2Lt	Second-Lieutenant
3D	3-Dimensional
3 Para	3rd Battalion The Parachute Regiment Battle Group
AAR	After-Action Report
ADZ	Afghan Development Zone
AH	Attack Helicopter
AK	Avtomat Kalashnikova (Russian-designed automatic rifle)
ANA	Afghan National Army
ANP	Afghan National Police
ANSF	Afghan National Security Forces
AO	Area of Operation
BG	Battle Group
BGen	Brigadier-General
C-17	Boeing Globemaster III Strategic Airlifter
CADPAT	Canadian Disruptive Pattern
Capt	Captain
CAS	Close Air Support
CAT	Combat Application Tourniquet
CDS	Chief of Defence Staff
CEFCOM	Canadian Expeditionary Force Command
CENTCOM	Central Command
CF	Canadian Forces
CIDA	Canadian International Development Agency
CIMIC	Civil-Military Cooperation
CO	Commanding Officer
CoG	Centre of Gravity
Col	Colonel
CP	Command Post
Cpl	Corporal
C/S	Call Sign
CWO	Chief Warrant Officer
DFAIT	Department of Foreign Affairs and International Trade

EOD	Explosive Ordnance Detachment
ETT	Embedded Training Team
EW	Electronic Warfare
FAC	Foreign Affairs Canada
FOB	Forward Operating Base
FOO	Forward Observation Officer
FSG	Forward Support Group
G-Wagon	Geländewagen (Mercedes Light Utility Vehicle)
G19	1) Glock 19 (compact semi-automatic pistol designed by the Austrian company Glock GmbH)
	2) Vehicle in LCol Hope's convoy
Gen	General
GOA	Government of Afghanistan
HLS	Helicopter Landing Site
HLTA	Home Leave Travel Assistance
HQ	Headquarters
HSS	Health Services Support
HUMINT	Human Intelligence
HVT	High Value Target
ICOM	Intercepted Communications
IED	Improvised Explosive Device
IFF	Identification, Friend or Foe
ISAF	International Security Assistance Force
ISR	Intelligence/Surveillance/Reconnaissance
ISTAR	Intelligence, Surveillance, Target Acquisition and Reconnaissance.
JDAM	Joint Direct Attack Munition
JSOA	Joint Special Operations Area
JTAC	Joint Target and Aerospace Control
KAF	Kandahar Airfield
KIA	Killed in Action
LAV	Light Armoured Vehicle
LCol	Lieutenant-Colonel
LOC	Lines of Communication
Lt	Lieutenant
LUVW	Light Utility Vehicle Wheeled

M777	155-mm Howitzer towed artillery piece
Maj	Major
MCpl	Master Corporal
MEDEVAC	Medical Evacuation
MEWT	Mobile Electronic Warfare Team
MP	Military Police
NATO	North Atlantic Treaty Organization
Nyala	African-designed RG-31 model multi-purpose mine-protected vehicle commonly used by peacekeeping and security forces.
NCM	Non-Commissioned Member (denotes all ranks from Private to Chief Warrant Officer inclusive)
NCO	Non-Commissioned Officer (denotes all ranks from Corporal to Sergeant inclusive)
ND	Negligent Discharge
NSE	National Support Element
OC	Officer Commanding
OEF	Operation Enduring Freedom
OPCON	Operational Control
PDC	Provincial Development Committee
PKM	Pulemyot Kalashnikova Modernizirovanniy (Russian-designed general purpose machine gun)
Pte	Private
PO	Performance Objective
PPCLI	Princess Patricia's Canadian Light Infantry
PPE	Personal Protective Equipment
PPIED	Pressure-Plate-Activated Improvised Explosive Device
PRT	Provincial Reconstruction Team
PSYOP	Psychological Operations
QRF	Quick Reaction Force
RC-S	Regional Command South
RCMP	Royal Canadian Mounted Police
Recce	Reconnaissance
ROE	Rules of Engagement
RPG	Rocket-Propelled Grenade
RSM	Regimental Sergeant-Major
SF	Special Forces
Sgt	Sergeant

SSE	Sensitive Site Exploitation
SOP	Standard Operating Procedure
Tac	Tactical
TACSAT	Tactical Satellite Radio
TF	Task Force
TOC	Tactical Operations Centre
TTP	Tactics, Techniques and Procedures
TUAV	Tactical Unmanned Aerial Vehicle
UAV	Unmanned Aerial Vehicle
UK	United Kingdom
US AID	United States Agency for International Development
VBSIED	Vehicle-borne Suicide Improvised Explosive Device
VOR	Vehicle Off Road
VSA	Vital Signs Absent
WIA	Wounded in Action
WO	Warrant Officer
WOs	1) Plural of Warrant Officer
	2) A reference to Warrant Officers, Master Warrant Officers and Chief Warrant Officer collectively